SHERMAN'S 21 LAWS OF SPEAKING

HOW TO INSPIRE OTHERS TO ACTION

ROB SHERMAN, J.D.

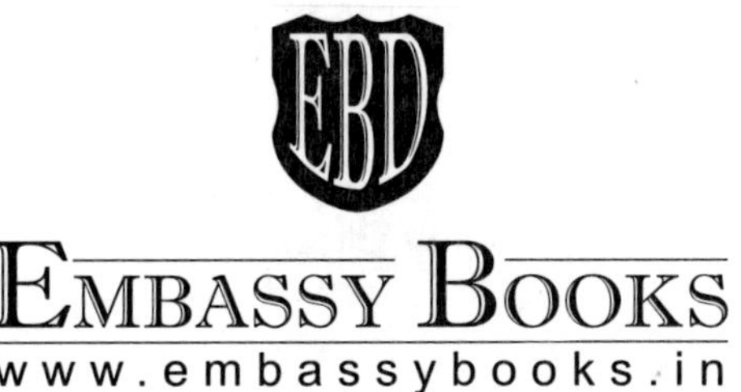

THIS BOOK IS DEDICATED
TO SUSAN AND ERIN AND TO MY PARENTS
FOR THEIR LOVE AND SUPPORT

SHERMAN'S 21 LAWS OF SPEAKING

First Indian Print: 2005

This edition licensed by arrangement with:
EMBASSY BOOKS. LLC.
1626 38th Ave North
St. Petersburg, FL 33713 US
Tel: +1 727 369-0740

Published in India by :
EMBASSY BOOK DISTRIBUTORS
120, Great Western Building,
Maharashtra Chamber of Commerce Lane,
Fort, Mumbai - 400 023.
Tel : (+91-22) 22819546 / 32967415
Email : info@embassybooks.in
Website: www.embassybooks.in

ISBN 13: 978-81-88452-27-9

Printed & Bound in India by Quarterfold Printabilities., Navi Mumbai

CONTENTS

INTRODUCTION

Let's face it. Some people have the ability to hold an audience in the palm of their hand, while for others public speaking is a painful experience – for them and for their listeners.

I was only a high school student when I noticed that every once in a while a student speaker would make a dynamite presentation. I watched one student introduce a candidate for class president from a prepared speech. Then he suddenly stopped in the middle of a sentence, folded up his prepared text and began to speak about the candidate from his heart. It was extremely effective; the audience loved the spontaneity of the presentation.

In law school, I watched a few rising legal stars who not only knew the law but were able to convey their thoughts in a way that was distinctly more effective than other attorneys. I also saw excellent attorneys fail miserably in court as they attempted to work from a prepared script. It just didn't work. The truly great trial lawyers gave the impression that they were speaking from the soul, even if they knew their script word for word.

Over the years I came to realize that these individuals had an innate ability to understand the importance of connecting with an audience. Knowing the facts or the law was vital, but often not enough to capture the hearts of an audience – or a jury. The effective communicators usually did the best job for their clients.

As a young trial lawyer, I learned this lesson firsthand. I was representing a state agency as an assistant attorney general when I found myself up against a seasoned pro. I carefully studied the law and the facts of the case, but it wasn't enough. My opponent knew the case as well as I did, yet as he eloquently presented his position, I knew I was doomed. Although he was only arguing his case to an administrative judge, he still was able to persuade with tremendous power. I was no match for him. A jury would have loved him even more.

The best trial attorneys know that juries are persuaded by connecting with the individual jurors. The details of the case are important but frequently not the overriding issue for jurors. Whether it is a jury or the Junior League, the rules are the same. People want more than words read from a piece of paper. They want to connect with the speaker.

There's something else I learned. Just as written principles guide the legal profession, certain canons of communication, when followed, produce extraordinary results for all public speakers. That is why I have written *Sherman's 21 Laws of Speaking*.

SPEAKERS ARE LEADERS

The moment you rise to speak, you assume a position of leadership. It doesn't matter if you are standing before two, 2,000, or 20,000 people. The very essence of any presentation is to move others to action – to inspire change.

Great leaders are great communicators, yet not everyone can utter a phrase like Winston Churchill. Few of us can hold the attention of an audience like Colin Powell. And it's a rare person who can tell a story like Paul Harvey.

As you will discover, you don't have to be a media star or reside in the pages of our history books to make presentations with power and confidence. You can learn from these *power presenters* by simply following their examples.

Why should you be concerned about polishing your speaking abilities? Think about the individuals at the top of your profession and you'll no doubt find excellent presenters. Their success is tied to their ability to persuade. For example, a survey of engineering school faculty members found that 15 percent of an engineer's future success is dependent on his or her engineering skills, while 85 percent depends on *communication skills*.[1]

It's not only true of engineers, but of those in education, government, and business. Top leaders are also effective speakers.

John Graham of Graham Communications summed up the value of speaking in these terms: "Speaking, like writing, is valuable in business because it reflects an ability to think, analyze ideas, make judgments, develop arguments that command attention and organize information in a way that moves people to action."[2]

A Learned Skill

My experience in training executives to be effective presenters has reinforced the fact that many leaders who are *not* natural speakers have learned the techniques necessary to communicate forcefully. Their voices are not typical of the so-called "professional" speaker, yet they can captivate an audience. That's good news for those of us who do not have voices like Charlton Heston or James Earl Jones. What these leaders understand is that effective speaking is critical to their success at all levels.

This book is designed to help you become a *leadership speaker*:

- One who understands the relationship between speaking and leadership.
- One who looks for opportunities to enhance his or her executive abilities through speaking to groups.
- One who knows that making presentations is a fast track to the top of the career ladder.

One executive observed, "Just five minutes in front of the right audience can be worth more than a whole year behind your desk."

Whether you are a teacher, salesperson, attorney, politician or CEO, I invite you put these *21 Laws of Speaking* into practice. I believe they will significantly improve your ability to communicate and help you inspire others to action.

– Rob Sherman

SHERMAN'S LAW #1

GAIN COMMITMENT BY CONNECTING WITH YOUR AUDIENCE

I've asked many people during executive training sessions, "What are the qualities you admire most in a speaker?" The answers have included words such as "authentic," "passionate," "motivational," and "humorous." One person told me, "A good speaker relates to *my* problems and offers solutions."

The common thread found in most responses is that people want to *relate* to a speaker in a meaningful way. Terry Pearce, in *Leading Out Loud*, states, "The unmistakable conclusion of contemporary social research is that people are eager to commit. They are truly starved to connect with competent, trustworthy leaders."[1]

PEOPLE ARE ...TRULY STARVED TO CONNECT WITH COMPETENT, TRUST-WORTHY LEADERS

- TERRY PEARCE

The *connection* is the major distinction between an ordinary speech and one that has the potential to make a difference in someone's life.

Remember, the ultimate purpose of most presentations is to move your audience toward a decision.

THE BOTTOM LINE

You should not concern yourself about what you receive as a result of the speaking engagement – whether it be remuneration or respect. You need to ask, "What am I going to *give?* Will my listeners take away something worthwhile?"

YOUR MESSAGE CAN TOUCH AND HEAL IF YOU ALLOW IT TO

– LILLY WALTERS

Every person seated before you has a need, and you have the opportunity to fill it. Lilly Walters, in her exceptional book, *Secrets of Successful Speakers*, suggests that you imagine that the minds of your audience are hurting. Says Walters, "Your message can touch and heal if you allow it to."

Audience benefit is the bottom line. That is what must guide every addition, deletion and revision you make to your program.

From the beginning, tell your listeners how and why they will greatly benefit from what they are about to hear. In essence, you're saying, "Listen up! Here is vital, important information for you!"

As author Morton Orman says, "Some-times we get so caught up in the presentation that we forget that our purpose is to provide value to the audience."[2]

THE CREDIBILITY FACTOR

Do your listeners see you as authentic and credible?

Lee Glickstein, founder of Transformational Speaking, believes that "authenticity is . . . one of the most effective leadership tools around. In an age of cynicism and distrust, it is one of the few things that inspires people to action." And he adds, "What we say doesn't count for much if people don't believe us, or if they don't think that we believe ourselves. Today, enlightened business leaders build trust and get results by revealing their authentic selves and setting an inspired example."[3]

If you want to check your credibility, test your material on your kids. My 10-year-old daughter, Erin, recently gave this sage advice: "If you have something to say, say it. If not, shut up!"

You'll never motivate others unless you believe in yourself – and have total faith in what you are communicating. As author Granville Toogood states in *The Articulate*

IF YOU HAVE SOMETHING TO SAY, SAY IT. IF NOT, SHUT UP!

– ERIN SHERMAN, AGE 10

Executive, "Once you stand for something, you have set yourself apart from every speaker – even if you may think you're not a particularly good speaker yourself."[4]

WORD POWER

On a cross-country flight, I was seated next to a college professor who told me about his speaking activities during the Vietnam war era while he was a graduate student at Stanford University. He believed the anti-war movement needed to take its case to the masses, so he would speak anytime – anywhere.

"Can you imagine what it was like addressing a conservative Kiwanis Club about the anti-war movement – and what a bad idea it was to invade Cambodia?" he told me.

At the conclusion of his speech, which received limited applause, he noticed a man following him to his car, anxious to talk. Instead of showing signs of anger, the short, rotund elderly gentleman was smiling. The man approached him, pointing his finger, saying, "You know, son, I didn't agree with what you said in there, but you had style. And I respect that in a person."

"IF YOU CAN SPEAK LIKE THAT TO A GROUP OF KIWANIS MEMBERS, YOU CAN DO JUST ABOUT ANYTHING."

To his astonishment, the man began to talk about his lucrative siding business and how he didn't have any heirs to take it over.

Amazingly, the stranger was offering the student an opportunity to work for him and ultimately own the business. "If you can speak like that to a group of Kiwanis members, you can do just about anything," he exclaimed.

The graduate student kindly refused the offer, but he never forgot the man's kindness. "I also learned the power of the spoken word," he told me.

ROB'S REMINDERS

- Connect with your audience by giving them something of value.
- Your objective is to provide benefits.
- People have needs that you have the opportunity to fill.
- Believe in yourself and your message.
- Authenticity is a critical leadership tool.
- When you stand for something, you set yourself apart.

WHEN YOU STAND FOR SOMETHING, YOU SET YOURSELF APART

SHERMAN'S LAW #2

SPEAK WITH PASSION AND YOU'LL INSPIRE OTHERS

On March 20, 1775, Patrick Henry stood before the Virginia Assembly in Richmond and delivered what many have proclaimed to be the greatest speech in the history of America. Why was it so memorable? The address was filled with fervor and emotion.

The great patriot concluded his oration with these stirring words: "Is life so dear, or peace so sweet, as to be purchased at the price of chains and slavery? Forbid it, Almighty God! I know not what course others may take; but as for me, give me liberty, or give me death!"[1]

ONLY PASSIONS, GREAT PASSIONS, CAN ELEVATE THE SOUL TO GREAT THINGS

– DENIS DIDEROT

Powerful, memorable addresses are the result of the speaker's deep passion for his or her subject. It is virtually impossible to inspire others if you are not personally committed.

WHAT'S THE VERDICT?

I once watched an attorney give his opening statement during a trial. He spoke in a monotone voice, droning on and on about what the evidence would show. There was no life, no persuasion.

I could sense the jurors thinking, "If this isn't important to him, why should it be important to me?"

Remember, every audience is a jury – voting up or down on your effectiveness.

Your objective is to change minds and move hearts. As professional speaker Janet Fox once said to me, "Leaders understand that they don't just sell widgets."

LEADERS UNDER-STAND THAT THEY DON'T JUST SELL WIDGETS

– JANET FOX

TRANSFER IT!

It is not enough to speak with passion and enthusiasm – you must *transfer* those same feelings to your audience. That's why it's vital that you put the *laws of speaking* into action. The transference comes through your voice, your gestures, your body movement and your mastery of platform skills.

Inspiration is contagious – even more so in the hands of a capable leader.

Nido Qubein advises, "If something is wonderful, say it like it's wonderful; if something is sad, say it like it's sad; if something is important, say it like it's important."[2]

FEELINGS OF THE HEART

Perhaps the quickest way to decrease speech anxiety is to allow the emotion of the subject to fill your heart. As speaker Roxanne Emmerich says, "When you are so committed to the meaning of your message you can't contain yourself, there is no energy left for being nervous."

Can you *always* make a passionate speech? No. If your assignment is to give a data-filled, informative session, follow the laws of good speaking and stick to the numbers. You can save enthusiasm for another time.

WHEN YOU ARE SO COMMITTED TO THE MEANING OF YOUR MESSAGE YOU CAN'T CONTAIN YOURSELF, THERE IS NO ENERGY LEFT FOR BEING NERVOUS

– ROXANNE EMMERICH

RAISE THE TEMPERATURE

Here's what I have learned by watching the pros. They know how to grab the attention of their audience early, yet they don't overplay their emotional cards during the first half of their presentation. They let the speech *simmer* and build to a boil - slowly raising the temperature along the way. Then, *wham!* At the conclusion, everything is bubbling over - the conviction, the intensity and the power.

Speaking coach Martha Burgess says, "It's energy that makes you visible, that gives you presence. It's called 'performance energy,' and is the basis of dynamic leadership."

You cannot fake enthusiasm; it must rise to the surface from deep within. There's no substitute for that fire-in-the-belly passion that causes your audience to *feel* something.

It's not what you think, it's what you believe.

THE DIFFERENCE BETWEEN ONE MAN AND ANOTHER IS NOT MERE ABILITY – IT IS ENERGY

– THOMAS ARNOLD

ROB'S REMINDERS

- Memorable addresses are the result of a deep passion.
- Your objective is to change minds and hearts.
- Inspiration and enthusiasm are contagious.
- Let the emotional pace of your speech *build.*
- Performance energy is the basis of dynamic leadership.
- It's not what you think, it's what you *believe*.

SHERMAN'S LAW #3

YOUR BEST SPEAKING STYLE IS YOUR OWN

One of the most widely accepted myths of public speaking is that a speaker must take on a different *persona* while on the platform. Nothing could be further from the truth.

If you think you must dramatically change your style when standing before a group, you are making a serious error that will perpetuate your speaking fear. After all, if you have to transform yourself on the platform, how can you possibly relax and "be yourself?"

The good news is that average people with natural speaking voices can deliver outstanding presentations. Who are the most successful speakers? Those who bond with an audience by being themselves and speak in a normal, down-to-earth manner.

AVERAGE PEOPLE WITH NATURAL SPEAKING VOICES CAN DELIVER OUTSTANDING PRESEN–TATIONS

IF YOU ARE MERELY PUTTING ON A SHOW FOR THE PURPOSE OF APPEARING TO BE A SHOWMAN, YOUR AUDIENCE WILL KNOW IT

– KIRK KIRKPATRICK

IT'S NOT AN ACT

Public speaking must never be viewed as an exhibition or an "act." As speaker Kirk Kirkpatrick says, "If you are merely putting on a show for the purpose of appearing to be a showman, your audience will know it and resent it, and they will turn you off."[1]

Here's another danger. When you think of public speaking as a "performance," anxiety and nervousness begin to build. That apprehension, however, can be quickly dispelled. Author Lee Glickstein says, "When we shift from performance to relationship-oriented speaking, relating one-to-one . . . a miracle happens – the fear is gone! We never again have to be afraid in front of groups."[2]

DON'T IMITATE

It is futile to mimic other professional speakers. While you can gain valuable insight by watching others and will learn from the tools they use to enhance their effectiveness, you should never attempt to copy them. It just doesn't work.

I once conducted a program with a doctor who, by nature, was a quiet man – and brilliant. We worked well together because our styles contrasted. His presentation was more subdued than mine, and his wit and professionalism were constantly at the fore-front. Then one day he attempted to emulate my up-tempo style. He thought that *all* professional speakers were more energetic than he was. It was a disaster. His *forced* style made him feel uncomfortable and resulted in a less-attentive audience.

The doctor soon reverted to his natural, well-received approach.

Speaking coach Martha Burgess observes, "True power comes from within. You need to live up to your potential instead of imitating someone else's."

YOU NEED TO LIVE UP TO YOUR POTENTIAL INSTEAD OF IMITATING SOMEONE ELSE'S.

– MARTHA BURGESS

THE HOLTZ APPROACH

Football coach Lou Holtz, one of America's most sought after platform personalities, pokes fun at the fact that he is not a "professional speaker" who articulates every word properly. He takes a *down-home* approach that establishes instant rapport.

At an annual convention of the National Speakers Association, Coach Holtz was surrounded by "fans" (professional speakers) after his address to the membership. What made him the darling of the NSA convention? He connected with the audience by being himself, not by adopting someone else's speaking style.

YOU'RE EQUAL!

Never, ever "talk down" to an audience or assume you are somehow superior. The opposite is also true. Don't come across with false humility or become apologetic. The only assumption you should make is that you are *equal* with those in front of you – and have something worth sharing.

The "commune" in *communicate* should tell you the importance of being on the same wavelength.

NO ONE WANTS TO ATTEND A LECTURE, YET MOST EVERYONE ENJOYS A CONVERSATION

– TONY JEARY

TEAR DOWN THE WALLS

Speak conversationally – it will break down any barriers that exist between you and your audience.

Is there really a great difference between talking while you are sitting down or standing behind a lectern? Only in your mind. The objective is to communicate as naturally as possible. Remember, effective speaking is *simple* speaking.

Tony Jeary, author of *Inspire Any Audience*, asks, "Why do presentations have a reputation for being boring? Because presenters tend to lecture. No one wants to attend a lecture, yet most everyone enjoys a conversation."[3]

Regardless of your speaking skills, you can connect with an audience. Develop your own comfortable style and stick with it.

ROB'S REMINDERS

- Don't dramatically change your speaking style.
- Public speaking is not an exhibition or an "act."
- It's futile to imitate other speakers.
- The conversational approach removes barriers.
- Aim to be on the same wave-length as your audience.
- Effective speaking is *simple* speaking.

EFFECTIVE SPEAKING IS SIMPLE SPEAKING

SHERMAN'S LAW #4

NEVER BEGIN A SPEECH WITHOUT A GOAL

In an executive training session, the president of a computer software company asked me, "What's the most important part of a presentation?"

"That's easy," I responded. "Always begin and end with your purpose in mind."

"Doesn't everybody know that?" he questioned.

"I certainly wish they did!" I answered.

I'm sure you too have fidgeted and squirmed through speeches that drifted far from the announced topic. You've wondered, "Does the speaker have an outline?" or, "Where is this train headed?"

What's the cause of such a disaster? Author Tony Jeary believes, "Too many presenters like to jump in and start developing the nitty-gritty details of a presentation before they've carefully considered where they're going and why."[1]

ALWAYS BEGIN AND END WITH YOUR PURPOSE IN MIND

WITHOUT A PURPOSE, NOTHING SHOULD BE DONE

- MARCUS AURELIUS

It's been said, "If you don't know where you're going, you will never recognize your destination when you arrive." It is true of explorers, entrepreneurs and even speakers.

What is the purpose of your presentation?

- To inform?
- To entertain?
- To teach a specific skill?
- To persuade?
- To change an attitude?
- To motivate or inspire?
- To call to action?

YOUR PURPOSE STATEMENT

Before you begin preparing your address, write a clear, short statement that details your purpose and objective. You may never use those exact words in the speech, yet they will be the magnet that pulls every thought, concept, quote, anecdote or visual illustration into focus.

What do you want people to do as a result of your presentation? What impact will this make on their lives?

Here's an easy way to arrive at your *purpose statement*. Finish this sentence: "As a result of my address, I want those in my audience to ________________________."

As you organize your speech, look at every point and subpoint. Ask yourself, "Does it really support my goal?"

Delete every item that doesn't belong and revise anything that is unclear.

THE "WHO CARES?" TEST

After completing the outline, go back over each major point and ask this question: *"Who cares?"* If the answer is "I'm not sure *anybody* cares," either remove the section or rework it into something you're convinced the audience needs.

If you can't figure out why people should care about a point you are making, how can you expect others to benefit from your message?

BE A RIFLE

To avoid a "so what?" response, make certain your purpose is *significant* – that is, that it increases your listeners' knowledge or improves their personal welfare.

Your purpose must also be *precise.* Limit yourself to *one* objective – not two, three or more. Be a rifle, not a shotgun.

If your goal is complex or overwhelming, you will lose your listeners before you are even introduced! A 40-minute presentation is no place for "The Historical, Sociological and Philosophical Impact of Rock Music."

TO AVOID A "SO WHAT?" RESPONSE, MAKE CERTAIN YOUR PURPOSE IS SIGNIFICANT AND PRECISE

NARROW YOUR OBJECTIVE

Here's an example of how to arrive at a specific goal for your speech.

Topic: The United Way Needs You.

IF YOU DON'T KNOW WHAT YOU WANT TO DO, IT'S HARDER TO DO IT

– MALCOLM FORBES

General Purpose: To persuade.

The Purpose Narrowed: To promote a definite action.

Specific Purpose: To motivate the audience to contribute to the United Way campaign.

ROB'S REMINDERS

- Define the objective of your presentation.
- Write a clear purpose statement.
- Apply the "Who cares?" test.
- Be certain your purpose is significant and precise.
- Narrow your objective.
- Always begin and end with your purpose in mind.

SHERMAN'S LAW #5

STICK WITH YOUR THEME – IT'S A ROADMAP TO UNDERSTANDING

After you have developed your goal, you have to provide your audience with a theme – a roadmap to understanding that drives them toward the target.

Your goal is the end result. Your theme is the primary force that motivates your listeners to adopt your objective as theirs. When developing your theme, keep a notebook with you. Write ideas and phrases on your topic until the words start exploding off the pages.

In your actual presentation, repeat and reinforce the central idea again and again. Drive the message home so the audience will never forget it.

REPEAT AND REINFORCE THE CENTRAL IDEA AGAIN AND AGAIN

MOST PEOPLE RECALL MUCH MORE ABOUT A SPEAKER'S PERSONALITY AND STYLE OF DELIVERY THAN THE CONTENT

A SINGLE IDEA

I've asked colleagues, "What do you remember about the last program you attended?"

Most people recall much more about a speaker's personality and style of delivery than the content. Sometimes they will recount a specific story or slice of humor, but rarely can they tell you about the *substance* of the speech. Why? Because so few speakers know how to present a powerful single concept and make it memorable.

Cavett Robert, National Speakers Association founder and a platform legend, gave one speech several thousand times: "You Can't Heat an Oven with Snowballs."

Every anecdote, illustration and idea was aimed at motivating the listener to add enthusiasm to his or her life.

FOCUS! FOCUS! FOCUS!

Two things will happen when you pick a major theme and stick to it:

First, your audience will feel comfortable with where you are leading them – they will appreciate the fact that you have a sense of direction.

Second, you'll be brimming with self-confidence by being an expert on your subject.

For example, if you are giving a 20-minute speech and your purpose is to motivate the audience to contribute to a charitable campaign, you may define your theme in these terms: "Giving to this charity creates new jobs that directly benefit the community." Your presentation will continually reinforce that theme, and you will delete extraneous information that does not support this central idea.

A CEO may make a keynote speech with a goal of demonstrating to her employees that world competition provides enormous opportunities to the company for growth. What is the central theme supporting the goal? It is her belief that the quality of her employees and the company's commitment to technology will provide this company with a competitive edge if everyone remains committed to the mission, vision and strategic plan.

As a child, you probably did the experiment involving converging the rays of the sun through a magnifying glass until some dry leaves began to burn. That should be your objective in preparing your speech. Focus! Focus! Focus! As ice skater Tai Babilonia says, "If you don't concentrate, you'll end up on your rear."

IF YOU DON'T CONCENTRATE, YOU'LL END UP ON YOUR REAR

– TAI BABILONIA

BE A SPECIALIST

The most successful people on the professional speaking circuit are not generalists – they're *specialists*.

What's the secret to becoming a world-class authority on a given topic? Decide to know more and more about less and less. Make it your objective to become so knowledgeable about your specific topic that you are recognized as one of the leading experts in your field.

IMMERSING YOURSELF IN YOUR SUBJECT ALLOWS YOU TO SPEAK WITH POWER

- DOTTIE WALTERS

Dottie Walters, a guru to professional speakers, says, "Immersing yourself in your subject allows you to speak with power."[1]

This is great news for the CEO. Once the CEO steps on the platform, he or she is already viewed as an expert.

VALUE EVERY WORD

Most speakers have much more to say than time will allow. So they decide to use the "hang on to your hats" approach and begin a rapid-fire delivery.

Your audience can process only so much information. If you question the content – or it is the slightest bit extraneous – remove it. Treat every word of your address as essential to your objective and valuable to your listener.

A SHORT, STRAIGHT PATH

Think of speech preparation as constructing a highway. Would you deliberately design detours, sharp curves and barricades? No. You want travelers to arrive at their destination in the shortest time possible. As author Andre Gide observes, "A straight path never leads anywhere except to the objective."

A STRAIGHT PATH NEVER LEADS ANYWHERE EXCEPT TO THE OBJECTIVE

-ANDRE GIDE

ROB'S REMINDERS

- Develop a powerful single idea.
- Repeat and reinforce your central theme.
- A sense of direction makes the audience comfortable.
- Being an expert on your topic produces self-confidence.
- Focus! Focus! Focus!
- Construct a short, straight path to your destination.

SHERMAN'S LAW #6

THE MORE YOU KNOW YOUR AUDIENCE, THE MORE THEY'LL WANT TO KNOW YOU

Discovering the needs, desires and fears of your audience is essential if you want to "ring the bell" as a speaker. There is no better way to connect.

The advice of noted author and lecturer Stephen Covey applies equally to one-on-one interactions and group presentations: "Seek first to understand – then to be understood." It is extremely difficult to build a strong rapport with an audience until you get on their same wavelength.

SEEK FIRST TO UNDERSTAND - THEN TO BE UNDERSTOOD

- STEPHEN COVEY

FIVE BASIC DESIRES

Psychologists have identified dozens of factors that drive human behavior and performance. In most audiences, however, you'll find these five basic desires:

1. *The desire to know.*
   What can I learn as a result of attending this presentation? How will it add value to my education?
2. *The desire for wealth.*
   Will the information I receive produce financial benefits either now or in the future? Is it a wise investment of my time?
3. *The desire to change.*
   Can this knowledge help me escape an unwanted behavior pattern? Will it open doors for personal transformation?
4. *The desire to acquire a skill.*
   Will I become competent or proficient in my present job or at a new task?
5. *The desire for happiness.*
   Is the information I learn personally fulfilling? Will it increase my well-being?

MY GREATEST STRENGTH AS A CONSULTANT IS TO BE IGNORANT AND TO ASK A FEW QUESTIONS

- PETER DRUCKER

ASK THE RIGHT QUESTIONS

When the president of a corporation makes a presentation to internal stakeholders, you can rest assure he or she will have a firm grasp on the inner workings of the organization. If not, that person will soon be looking for a new job!

Finding the motivation of an *external* audience is more difficult – yet much easier to determine than you think. All it takes is asking the right questions.

For example, a health-care professional who is about to speak to the local Rotary Club can ask the meeting planner for a club directory that will provide the names, occupations and corporate addresses of those likely to attend.

The presenter may want to contact several club members and ask a few specific questions related to the topic. Or, a simple survey can extract the needed responses.

Other time-efficient ways to profile your audience include looking at the home pages of companies on the Internet, or sending an e-mail questionnaire to those who will attend your session.

KNOWLEDGE IS POWER AND IT COMES FROM ASKING QUESTIONS – TONS OF THEM

– JO ROBBINS

ARRIVE EARLY

Some speakers personally interview two or three attendees in preparation for a program and then refer to those individuals during the presentation.

If you're speaking at a convention, try to arrive a day early and talk with as many participants as possible. Also attend other sessions to get a feel for the event.

REQUEST INPUT

A potentially dangerous, yet extremely effective approach is to leave a slot open at the beginning of your program to ask, "What burning issues would you like me to cover today?" or, "What are your expectations for this program?"

The "plus" is that you can tailor the speech to immediate needs. The "minus" is that you may look unprepared – or mention so many topics that half the audience will be disappointed. (Of course, you can always say, "I'll be happy to talk with you personally after the program if there's not time for your topic.")

WHAT TO ASK

"TELL ME ABOUT THE AUDIENCE. WHAT ARE THEIR NEEDS, DESIRES AND FEARS?"

Professional speakers always phone the program chairperson and ask, "Tell me about the audience. What are their needs, desires and fears?"

Some take the time to send a printed questionnaire to the meeting planner to learn as much as possible about the audience.

Here are six important things you need to know:

1. What is the makeup of the audience? Top- level executives? Mid-level managers? New employees?

2. What current challenges and problems facing the organization will I be addressing?
3. Are there any industry buzzwords or language in current use I need to know?
4. Is this a volunteer audience, or are they required to attend?
5. Are there any topics or issues I should avoid?
6. What do you feel people will want to take away from this presentation?

MORE QUESTIONS

You may also want to know these things about your audience:

■ Level of education. ■ Exposure to programs similar to yours. ■ Cultural backgrounds. ■ Age range. ■ Male/ female ratio. ■ Does anyone have a hidden agenda? ■ Why are they interested in this topic?

GREAT COOPERATION

My friend Jo Robbins, author of *High Impact Presentations,* sends a detailed questionnaire in advance to the coordinator of any workshop, seminar or course she is about to present. Observes Robbins, "The cooperation I receive often goes beyond what is expected. In addition to the written responses, I've had executives call me to share detailed insights into situations the company and certain employees were

"ARE THERE ANY TOPICS OR ISSUES I SHOULD AVOID?"

currently facing."[1]

Never underestimate the importance of this law of speaking: *The more you know your audience, the more they'll want to know you.*

Rob's Reminders

- Know the needs, desires and fears of your audience.
- Use questionnaires to learn about your listeners in advance.
- Arrive early and talk with participants.
- Ask if there are topics you should avoid.
- Find out what people want to take home from your presentation – then give it to them.

SHERMAN'S LAW #7

NEVER READ YOUR SPEECH!

You can practice your presentation until it becomes second nature. You may even memorize your speech. However, there is one rule you must not break: *Never, never read your speech.*

What are the results of reading? It's been said, "The last time someone deliberately read to you, it was your mother, and she was trying to put you to sleep."

"THE LAST TIME SOMEONE DELIBERATELY READ TO YOU, IT WAS YOUR MOTHER, AND SHE WAS TRYING TO PUT YOU TO SLEEP"

Speakers who read a presentation will never connect with the audience. Even worse, their speech will likely be forgotten as quickly as the session is over.

A STARTLED MAYOR

I once heard about a big-city mayor who hired a young speech writer and became so dependent on him that he would not even proofread the copy – he would just start reading.

Unfortunately, the speech writer felt he was underpaid and under-appreciated. One afternoon, at a Rotary Club meeting, as the mayor was well into his address, he turned to page three and stopped dead in his tracks. At the top of the page were these words: "Okay, big guy. You're on your own. My resignation is effective immediately!"

"CANNED" OR IMPROMPTU

You may wonder, "If I'm not supposed to read my speech, why do I see world leaders sticking to a script or reading from a teleprompter?" Certainly, there are times when a speaker – knowing the words will be reported and analyzed in the media – will speak from a prepared text. Unless you are in that category, forget about reading.

IMPROMPTU, OFF-THE-CUFF ANSWERS RESULT IN A SPEAKER WHO IS MORE ANIMATED, HUMOROUS AND CAPTIVATING

One of the most memorable moments of recent political conventions was when Elizabeth Dole left the podium and walked through the audience – delivering her address without notes. It was both riveting and effective.

The next time you watch a presidential press conference, notice the difference between the "canned," stilted opening remarks versus the responses during the question-answer session. You'll see clearly that impromptu, off-the-cuff answers result in a speaker who is more animated, humorous and captivating.

THE "THREE-STEP" METHOD

What glues so many speakers to the written text? *Fear!*

It is natural to be anxious and feel the adrenaline pumping before beginning your speech. Some speakers, however, write out every word and cling to their texts like children clutching a mother's skirt. They are nervous about losing their train of thought or "freezing" on the platform.

How do we neutralize these fears and give a memorable presentation – *without reading*? Great keynote speakers are usually great "keyword" speakers. They arrive at their destination by carefully following this "three-step" method of preparation:

- *Step one:* Write your speech completely – word for word.
- *Step two:* From the finished product, make an outline.
- *Step three:* Create a "keyword" outline, choosing words that will remind you of the content in each main point.

Since eye contact is so important, avoid the temptation to read complete phrases.

GREAT KEYNOTE SPEAKERS ARE USUALLY GREAT "KEYWORD" SPEAKERS

FROM YOUR HEART

IT TAKES ONLY A SPLIT SECOND TO GLANCE DOWN – AND DELIVER THE MATERIAL FROM YOUR HEART

See your notes as a vital part of your presentation, not an escape hatch in case your mind suddenly goes blank. When you know your material, the keyword outline is all you need. It takes only a split second to glance down, look at the word, and deliver the material from your heart.

Some speakers draw symbols or pictures on their note cards in place of keywords. Let's say your speech includes a point about the dangers of violence on television. You might want to draw a gun on a TV screen.

If it gives you reassurance, go ahead and write out the first two or three phrases of your speech on a note card. Don't plan to read these words. *Memorize* them. Just knowing they are available on the card can boost your confidence.

The only time you may want to read from a note card or a sheet of paper is when referring to a detailed statistic or when delivering a quote that must be exact.

UNDETECTED NOTES

An audience handout containing the outline of your presentation can become your lecture notes. Your copy will be an "annotated" version, complete with keywor-ds and reminders. The audience will *expect* you to look at your notes, since they are following along.

Visual aids can also replace your note cards. Some speakers use either a flip chart, overhead projector or LCD projector. The headings and subheadings are not only for the audience, they are cues for the speaker.

When you glance at the handout or the visual, so will your listeners. It reinforces the message and helps maintain maximum eye contact.

EIGHT KEYS

Here are eight keys for more effective use of notes:

1. Use 4x6" cards or an 8 ½ x 11" sheet of paper. Be sure you can easily see your keywords while the card or paper is on the lectern. My personal preference is to use key words in 18-point type on a sheet of paper.
2. Number your pages or notes – in case you drop them.
3. Use only one side for notes. It's far less confusing.
4. Don't worry about glancing at your notes when necessary – at least it shows your listeners that you are prepared. But bring your eyes quickly back to the audience.
5. Review your keywords just before the speech. Be sure each word reminds you of the complete point you need to make.
6. Don't fumble with your notes. Keep them on the lectern.

PRACTICE UNTIL YOU FEEL COMFORT-ABLE MOVING AWAY FROM THE LECTERN. STAY ANIMATED.

7. Practice until you feel comfortable moving away from the lectern. Stay animated. Although you may occasionally glance at your notes, consider using annotated handouts.
8. Here's a trick used by the pros. They glance at their notes only when they make a sweeping gesture or move their body. The audience is looking at the movement – and rarely notices the speaker's eyes referring to the notes.

PREPARE, REHEARSE AND MEMORIZE, BUT DO NOT READ!

ROB'S REMINDERS

- Never, never, read your speech. Prepare, rehearse and memorize, but do not read!
- Use the *keyword* method for notes.
- Symbols and pictures can become keywords.
- Handouts and visual aids can become your notes.
- Review the keywords just before your speech.
- Keep your eyes on the audience, not on your notes.

SHERMAN'S LAW #8

PRACTICE – THEN PRACTICE AGAIN!

Great speakers rehearse their presentations again and again until they can practically give their speeches in their sleep! Many practice it so many times they actually have it memorized, yet that was not their original goal. What's the result? They know the content so well that the audience is unaware that every word is committed to memory.

For most of us, memorization is unnecessary – but practice is essential. The more familiar you become with your material, the easier the words flow. The more comfortable you feel with your words, the more naturally you present your speech. That's why good speakers practice – and practice again.

THE PARADOX FACED BY EVERY PRESENTER IS THAT IT TAKES CONSIDERABLE PREPARATION IN ORDER TO BE SPONTANEOUS

– BOB GEROLD

THE SINGLE MOST IMPORTANT THING YOU CAN DO FOR SWEATY PALMS IS REHEARSE

– DAVID PEOPLES

David Peoples, who has trained more than 8,000 IBM salespeople, says,"The single most important thing you can do for sweaty palms is *rehearse*. The second most important thing you can do for sweaty palms is *rehearse*. Guess what the third thing is?"[1]

"IT LOOKS SO EASY!"

Many executives become upset at themselves during coaching sessions for public speaking. Some are frustrated by the fact that they are frightened when they speak. As one CEO told me, "If I can successfully run a company, then I ought to be able to give a 20 minute speech!"

Others can't understand why it's difficult to really *master* public speaking. "This should be a breeze," I often hear. "It looks so easy when I see others do it!"

I address the executives' fear and frustration issues by asking, "How many times do you give major presentations each year?" It's usually a small number – perhaps five times.

Then I ask, "How often do you make major decisions at the company?"

"Practically every day!" is the common answer.

I respond, "So why do you expect your

speaking skills to be as developed as your decision-making ability? You just do not speak enough to overcome those fears."

Early in my own career I was so anxious about a presentation that my back "went out" during the program. I had to sit on a chair; otherwise I would not have finished the session.

One executive told me he was upset at himself because he was fearful of testifying before legislators at government hearings. "How often do you testify?" I asked. "Twice a year," he replied.

"If you testified each week, you'd lose your fear in a month," I answered. "Stop beating yourself up about your lack of perfection in an area you don't use daily."

STOP BEATING YOURSELF UP ABOUT YOUR LACK OF PERFECTION IN AN AREA YOU DON'T USE DAILY

SEE IT! HEAR IT!

Are you ready to begin rehearsing for a sure-fire event? Here's where to start:

See it! If you don't own a video camera, borrow one from a friend and start videotaping your practice sessions. You'll be shocked at how rapidly your speaking style will improve after you objectively review the tape. You will likely see nervous habits that you never knew you had.

Hear it! Make an audiocassette of your practice session and listen to it again and again. Immediately, you'll know if you are speaking too quickly or too slowly, or if some words are difficult to understand. You will hear mistakes in grammar and inappropriate "um's" and "ah's" that are quite easily removed from your presentation when you are totally aware of them. The audio sessions will help you zero in on content and vocal skills.

If you're not happy with what you see or hear, join the crowd. Your goal is to improve, not to wallow in self-criticism.

YOUR GOAL IS TO IMPROVE, NOT TO WALLOW IN SELF-CRITICISM

The experience is enlightening – and a little frightening.

The first time I watched a video of myself, I could not believe how much I moved on stage. It made me nervous just to watch myself "dance" around. How could the audience follow the program if my movements distracted them? Staying in one place and moving slowly on the platform was a struggle, but the video camera didn't lie. It told me what was necessary to change.

SIX PREPARATION STEPS

In addition to recording and observing your presentation on video and audio, here are six things you can do in preparation for your next speech:

1. ***Rehearse in front of a mirror.*** Don't just talk, watch yourself in action. Try to see how much eye contact you can maintain. Look at your gestures. Are you smiling when you should – and looking intense and serious when it is required?
2. ***Practice in front of a colleague and ask for an honest appraisal.*** You might feel uncomfortable giving a speech to an audience of one, yet it can greatly enhance your ultimate effectiveness. And don't hesitate to ask your spouse or close friend to give you an evaluation – that critique may be more candid than any you will hear.
3. ***Prepare with the exact same equipment you plan to use.*** If you're planning to use a flip chart or an overhead projector, set these up when you rehearse. If you're practicing without them, you are rehearsing only part of your presentation.
4. ***Practice in the same room where you will give the speech.*** If at all possible, visit the location where you will give the address and "get the feel" of the space. It's a great way to learn if you will need additional equipment – or how to set up the room. It will also increase your comfort level about the upcoming event.
5. ***Rehearse in front of a real audience.*** You may want to call a friend in a neighboring town or at another organization and say, "I have a new

PREPARE WITH THE EXACT SAME EQUIPMENT YOU PLAN TO USE

program and would really appreciate you putting a group together so that I can present it. There'll be no charge." At the event, make a video and hand out an evaluation form.

6. ***Join Toastmasters International.*** This will provide you with the necessary experience to push you toward your speaking goals. Tom Peters, in his book, *The Pursuit of Wow*, encourages leaders at all levels to join this outstanding organization. To find a Toastmasters chapter in your area, visit its Internet site listed in the Resources section at the end of this book.

You can master public speaking the exact same way a great musician makes it to Carnegie Hall: Practice, then practice again!

YOU CAN MASTER PUBLIC SPEAKING: PRACTICE, THEN PRACTICE AGAIN!

ROB'S REMINDERS

- Practice your speech until you feel comfortable with your words.
- Increase your speaking to decrease anxiety.
- Rehearse on videotape to improve your style.
- Practice on audiotape to improve your content and vocal skills.
- Get feedback from your friends and associates.
- Join Toastmasters International.

SHERMAN'S LAW #9

PREPARING YOUR ROOM IS PART OF PREPARING YOUR SPEECH

Before a 747 jetliner taxis down the runway, there's a lengthy checklist that receives the pilot's full attention.

As a speaker, you must also check details. Otherwise, your best-laid plans could result in disaster.

A successful speaking experience involves more than content preparation. You need to understand the impact of seating, lighting, sound, temperature – and unexpected disturbances.

IF YOU DON'T DO YOUR HOMEWORK, YOU WON'T MAKE YOUR FREE THROWS

- LARRY BIRD

SMART SEATING

Let's begin with the psychology of seating. If the chairs are portable and you can choose their arrangement, follow these important guidelines:

- Arrange the chairs wide rather than deep. Stay close to your audience.
- Consider roping off the back rows and forcing early arrivals to sit toward the front. Those who arrive late – even after the program begins – won't be so disruptive. Plus, your crowd won't be scattered.
- Set chairs as closely as possible to Where you stand. It allows a more intimate connection; you'll feel you are talking with friends instead of performing.

THEY WILL THINK, "WOW, THIS IS A SUCCESSFUL EVENT."

Some professional speakers even preset seating for about half the crowd they expect. The remaining chairs are stacked against the back wall. It's always exciting for an audience to see extra chairs being set up. They will think, "Wow, this is a successful event."

LET THERE BE LIGHT!

Here's how lighting can help brighten your presentation:

- Move the lectern so the

brightest light in the room shines on you. We are conditioned to look toward light.

- Ask yourself whether direct sunshine will bother people or affect your visuals in early morning or late afternoon. Prepare for every eventuality.
- Keep the lights bright – it adds excitement and retains the highest level of audience energy. Know how to dim the brightness for overheads or projectors, then increase the lighting when they are not in use. You may have to ask the facility coordinator to remove the light bulbs directly above the overhead.
- If there are windows behind you, cover them. You can't compete with cars or children playing.
- It is best to leave the lights on throughout the program. Turning them on and off can be very distracting.
- If there are light fixtures on the wall behind you, turn them off or you will look like a ghost and be hard to see.
- Before the program begins, ask someone to view you and your visual aids from every room angle to see if the lighting has maximum visual effect. It's better

KEEP THE LIGHTS BRIGHT – IT ADDS EXCITEMENT AND RETAINS THE HIGHEST LEVEL OF AUDIENCE ENERGY

to scrap the use of a particular visual aid than to present it with bad lighting. A "washed out" screen can result in a washed out presentation.

KEEP IT QUIET

Don't let external disturbances ruin your event.

- If you're speaking at a luncheon or a banquet, insist that the servers either clear the tables before you begin or finish their work later.
- Test the doors. If they make loud noises when they close, fix the annoyance with some appropriately placed masking tape – or seat someone near the door to control the problem.
- If there are doors behind you or toward the front, place signs on the outside saying, "Do not enter – meeting in progress."

INSIST THAT THE SERVERS EITHER CLEAR THE TABLES BEFORE YOU BEGIN OR FINISH THEIR WORK LATER

KEEP IT COOL

A warm room will lull your audience to sleep. Set the temperature at about 70 degrees – or even 68. Remember, a large crowd will heat up a room quickly. And don't forget the importance of ventilation. If you feel the air isn't circulating properly, open a window a few inches before the event begins.

Make sure you know the location of heating and cooling controls – or whom to call if you need immediate help.

KEEP IT CLOSE

Place the lectern close to the audience. Humorist Steve Kissell says, "A distance of 10' or 12' works well. Any more and you lose intimacy. Any less and you are in the 'speaker spit zone.'"[1]

A DISTANCE OF 10' OR 12' WORKS WELL. ANY MORE AND YOU LOSE INTIMACY. ANY LESS AND YOU ARE IN THE "SPEAKER SPIT ZONE."

– STEVE KISSELL

How important is it to check out the lectern? An executive of a major corporation was giving a speech to hundreds of senior executives. She was a petite woman and, unfortunately, she found herself behind a lectern that dwarfed her. She could have easily remedied this situation by requesting a riser – but she didn't. Instead, she opened with the question, "Can you see me? I can barely see you!" Her talk misfired because of the lack of advance planning.

CHECK IT PERSONALLY

Don't trust anyone to check the details. It's your event; you need to take complete control. Create a checklist tailored to your presentation.

- Arrive at least two – even three hours early. Many professionals arrive *one day* ahead of schedule.
- Test in advance every piece of equipment you will use.
- Do you know where the house light switches are located? Are they adjustable?
- Will you need a glass of water at the lectern?
- Take a few moments and sit in every section of the room. What is the perspective from these locations?
- Does the microphone work properly? (You should use one if there are more than 40 in the audience.)

BY FAILING TO PREPARE YOU ARE PREPARING TO FAIL

- BENJAMIN FRANKLIN

After you have taken every possible precaution, things may still go wrong. What should be your response? Smile, briefly recognize the problem and continue.

ROB'S REMINDERS

- Arrive at least two or three hours early or the night before.
- Bring a written checklist to the program.
- Be sure the brightest lights are focused on you.
- Avoid competing with noisy servers and slamming doors.
- Lower the temperature and keep people awake.
- Stay close to your audience.

SHERMAN'S LAW #10

RELAX BEFORE YOU SAY YOUR FIRST WORD

It's natural to have butterflies before an important event. As the old saying goes, "Your objective is to have the butterflies fly in formation!"

There are legendary stories of superstars who undergo extraordinary episodes of stage fright immediately before a performance. They've experienced blurred vision, nausea and throbbing headaches and often break out in a cold sweat - even after performing hundreds of times.

Most actors have learned to use relaxation techniques before walking on stage. Otherwise they attempt to suppress the anxiety and their performance suffers. And, if they continue to bottle up these apprehensions, their long-term health can be affected.

"YOUR OBJECTIVE IS TO HAVE THE BUTTERFLIES FLY IN FORMATION!"

THE HUMAN MIND IS A WONDERFUL THING – IT STARTS WORKING THE MINUTE YOU'RE BORN AND NEVER STOPS UNTIL YOU GET UP TO SPEAK IN PUBLIC

– ROSCOE DRUMMOND

Here are six techniques that can reduce your speaking anxieties:

1. Slow Breathing

People under stress tend to hold their breath or take fewer breaths. Also, their breathing is usually shallow, not taking air fully into their lungs.

Just before you walk to the lectern, take several deep breaths, allowing your diaphragm to expand completely. Breathe in for a count of five, hold for that same count, and exhale for a count of five. Suddenly, you'll feel more relaxed. You will also become more alert, since the process increases oxygen to your brain.

Many speakers find a quiet place before their presentation and breathe deeply for up to five minutes.

2. Calm Music

The hour before your speech can be extremely hectic – especially if unexpected problems suddenly surface. It's vital that you arrive early, complete the setup and find somewhere to be alone.

Bring along a stereo headset and some soothing music. Close your eyes and allow yourself to be "transported" to some distant location. Feel your body relaxing and your pulse rate slowing. Better yet, practice meditation.

3. Stress-Reducing Exercises

Physical exercise is a proven way to reduce prespeaking stress. For example:

- Shrug your shoulders upward and hold them for a count of five. Then roll them backward and forward.
- Try a few head rolls, slowly moving your head clockwise in a circle. Now reverse the procedure.
- Do some isometric exercises, pressing your hands together or pushing against a wall.
- Purchase a small "stress ball" and squeeze it before going on stage.
- Stretch your arms and legs – just a few seconds will work wonders.
- Lift your arms and stretch your back.
- Walk up and down a flight of stairs.
- Exercise your jaws. Open your mouth as wide as possible to relieve tension.

4. Visualization

Close your eyes and "see" yourself succeeding as a speaker – with the audience nodding in agreement. Hear yourself delivering a key point of your address. Picture your listeners laughing at your

CLOSE YOUR EYES AND "SEE" YOURSELF SUCCEEDING AS A SPEAKER – WITH THE AUDIENCE NODDING IN AGREEMENT

humor and applauding when you deliver a powerful concept.

5. The Right Mental Attitude

Drive out negative self-talk and stop dwelling on what could go wrong. Realize that, despite your anxiety, the audience is pulling for you. They want to have an enjoyable encounter, and they desire that you succeed. Why would they spend their time listening to you if they thought you would present a poor program? Enjoy the experience.

Barbara Braham, business coach and speaker, says, "If you aspire to be a wonderful speaker, get to know the place of silence within yourself. This is the place *speaking* comes from. Until you know this place, the best you can do is *talk*."

IF YOU ASPIRE TO BE A WONDERFUL SPEAKER, GET TO KNOW THE PLACE OF SILENCE WITHIN YOURSELF

– BARBARA BRAHAM

6. Talk with the Audience

Speak personally with as many people as you can from the audience before the program begins. Stand at the door and introduce yourself. Go around to each table and say hello. When you understand that your speech is just a continuation of this intimate contact with individuals, you'll realize there is no reason to be frightened. You are just talking with friends.

NOW YOU'RE READY!

You have just been introduced. You walk to the lectern and are about to say your first words. Wait! You have one more chance to unwind.

Pause for a few seconds and "take in" the audience. Establish eye contact with them. Take a deep breath, gently smile, and relax for a mo-ment. Now you are ready to begin!

A fellow speaker, Patrick Donadio, told me, "I once began a program so forcefully that a woman in the front row literally fell out of her seat." Patrick now starts more slowly so the audience will adjust to his speaking style.

In virtually every case, a person's fear of public speaking is unjustified. What's the worst that could happen? You could trip as you approach the stage, freeze, forget a sentence, drop your notes, stammer or shake. None of these things are fatal. The worst that *could* happen probably *won't.* Yet if it does, you can live through it.

Morton C. Orman, a medical doctor and popular speaker, says, "Even if you pass out, get tongue-tied, or say something stupid during your talk – they won't care! As long as they get something of value, they will be thankful."[1]

YOU SPEECH IS NOT ABOUT YOU. IT'S THE MESSAGE THAT COUNTS.

Realize that if you focus on how much you want the audience to understand the message, the spotlight is placed on them and your nervousness will subside. Your speech is not about you. It is the *message* that counts.

ROB'S REMINDERS

- Breathe slowly and deeply to reduce anxiety.
- Listen to soothing music or meditate before you speak.
- Try stress-reducing exercises.
- Visualize yourself succeeding as a speaker.
- Drive out negative self-talk.
- Pause before uttering your first word.

SHERMAN'S LAW #11

GRAB THEIR ATTENTION: START WITH A BANG!

It is tempting to commence your speech with words the audience expects, "Thank you. It's a pleasure being here today" and then ease slowly into your material. The danger is you may lose your audience before you ever begin.

The first 30 seconds are the "make or break" time for your presentation.

In reality, your speech begins before you walk to the lectern. That's why some speakers make sure that about 10 minutes before they are introduced, someone announces, "Our program will begin in a few minutes. If you need to use the restroom, or have some refreshments, do it now. Then get ready for an exciting event."

GRAB THEM EARLY, AND THEY'LL STICK BY YOU EVEN IF SOMETHING GOES WRONG LATER

- TONY JEARY

WRITE YOUR OWN INTRO

Getting off to a great start also includes the way you are introduced - and you can't take any chances. That's why you should write your own introduction.

Keep the intro to no more than 60 seconds - about 120 words. Type it in large letters on a sheet of paper and hand it to the person introducing you. Ask the introducer to practice reading the introduction while you listen.

What should the intro say? First, stress the benefits of the topic to the audience and then give your background. Be sure to note your credentials for speaking on this subject. It should end with a statement such as, "Ladies and gentlemen, please give a warm welcome to (Your Name)." You need to encourage lively applause as you walk to the lectern.

CONSIDER STARTING WITH A PROVOCATIVE STATEMENT, A RHETORICAL QUESTION, A SURPRISING FACT, OR A STORY RELATED TO YOUR TOPIC

If the introducer knows your qualifications well through personal experience, ask him or her to personalize the intro. Nothing establishes instant credibility like a well-respected member of the group telling a positive story about you as you take the stage.

OPENING OPTIONS

How should you begin? Consider starting with a provocative statement, a rhetorical question, a surprising fact, or a story related to your topic. For example, if you are giving a dinner speech as the newly elected president of the Widget Manufacturers of America, you might begin with the question, "Did you know that our association and MTV have much in common?" Then talk about the ways associations compete for member's time – just as MTV tries to attract viewers. You could continue with a discussion of the tremendous value people receive as association members.

Joan Detz, author of *How to Write and Give a Speech,* suggests starting with a "vivid comparison, customer comments, shareholder letters, witty quotations, professional endorsements, interesting definitions, one-liners, surveys, 'on this date' tidbits, geographical details, news headlines, employee profiles, references to popular culture, or historical anecdotes."[1]

Here are five examples of surefire openings:

1. **A startling statistic.** "Only eight percent of businesses are prepared for a computer systems failure." Or, "According to *Wealth Magazine*, professional advice has been wrong more than 75 percent of the time."

"HOW MANY OF YOU HAVE EVER SWUNG FROM A TREE LIKE TARZAN?"

– TOM ANTION

2. **An "outrageous" opening.** Noted speaker Tom Antion suggests beginning with an unusual question such as, "How many of you have ever swung from a tree like Tarzan?" Then continue with comments about it being "a jungle out there."
3. **A short anecdote.** If you are speaking on the importance of clear communication, you might open with the story of the teacher who took her second graders to an art museum. Looking at an abstract sculpture, a little boy asked, "What's that?" The teacher replied, "It's supposed to be a gal- loping horse." The boy said, "Well, why isn't it?"

   Better yet, begin with your own personal story that illustrates the main theme of your talk.
4. **An attention-getting question.** If you are speaking to a group of accountants, you could start with, "The late Malcolm Forbes claimed that 99 out of 100 questions could be answered by one word: *money*. Is that true in your organization?"
5. **A current headline.** Scan the newspapers of the last three days, and you're likely to spot a story directly related to your theme. Tie it to your opening, and the audience will think, "Good! Perhaps this isn't a canned speech!"

CAN YOU REDUCE THE MAJOR THEME OF YOUR SPEECH TO 10 SECONDS?

DISTILL YOUR "PURPOSE" IN 10 SECONDS

Be certain your opening is directly linked to the purpose of your presentation.

Some speakers make certain they can distill the major objective of the speech into a 10- second statement. That one phrase captures the absolute essence of their theme and is included in the first two minutes of their speech. If you are really struggling with an opening, try this: *Use your conclusion.* I'm sure you've heard the advice, "Begin with the end in mind." Start and finish by emphasizing the same major point.

While I don't recommend you memorize your entire address, you may want to memorize the first 30 seconds word for word; that way, you greatly reduce the odds of getting off to a poor start.

You may ask, "What happens if I mess up and everything goes wrong?" Simply pause, smile, look at your note cards and continue. Don't waste time with lengthy excuses.

Follow the advice of speech coach Ron Arden: "You must believe in what you say. Be poised – not much movement in the beginning. Take time with the audience."

A good start will launch you toward a great finish.

"WHAT HAPPENS IF I MESS UP AND EVERYTHING GOES WRONG?"

ROB'S REMINDERS

- Always write your own introduction.
- Consider memorizing the first 30 seconds of your presentation.
- Be sure your opening is tied to your purpose.
- Try beginning with a startling statistic, a short anecdote, or an attention-getting question.
- Consider linking your opening to current events or headlines.
- Condense your purpose into a 10 second statement.

SHERMAN'S LAW #12

ENERGIZE YOUR AUDIENCE: MAKE THEM DO SOMETHING

A common denominator of all great speakers is that they involve their audiences – almost instantly. In fact, people give a "thumbs down" to speakers who fail to create some kind of interaction.

Nido Qubein, noted platform personality and former president of the National Speakers Association, says, "The very first thing I do when I'm introduced is to get the audience into the act. I get them to do something with me."[1]

Your goal is to motivate listeners to "talk back" mentally.

THE VERY FIRST THING I DO WHEN I'M INTRODUCED IS TO GET THE AUDIENCE INTO THE ACT

—NIDO QUBEIN

Granted, some presenters go too far and attempt to engage audiences in trivial games that are inappropriate for the occasion. Yet there are proven methods of creating exciting involvement. Consider these eight options:

1. Ask to See Their Hands

Let's say you are giving a presentation on dealing with poor job performance. You might begin with, "I'd like to see the hand of everyone in this room who personally has had to fire someone. If you've had that experience, raise your hand." Make sure to raise your hand as you say this, as a subconscious suggestion.

THIS GETS THEIR BLOOD GOING, HAS THEM INVOLVED, AND MAKES FOR A FAR MORE ATTENTIVE AUDIENCE

– DON BLOHOWIAK

2. Get 'em on Their Feet

If appropriate to your theme, you'll get a surefire response by asking, "How many of you have served this country as a member of the armed forces? Will you please stand?" When they are on their feet, say, "Let's give these people a round of applause."

Professional speaker Don Blohowiak believes in energizing an audience. Says Don, "By asking meaningful questions, you can get people to stand and even raise one or both arms as an audience survey reply device. This provides you with feedback information that's relevant to your presentation content, and provides people in the audience with a legitimate excuse to get up and stretch."

Don also recommends a short series of survey questions that ask people to stand, sit, or extend their arms once or twice in rapid succession. "This gets their blood going, has them involved, and makes for a far more attentive audience."

3. Break into Groups

Consider asking your audience members to move into small groups for a short discussion on one of your main themes. For example, they can work on solving a specific problem or share successful aspects of their jobs.

Keep the discussion time short so you can get instant feedback. You can even have fun selecting a group spokesperson who will report by choosing:

✓ the individual with the last name closest to the end of the alphabet, or

✓ the person with a birthday nearest to today's date.

Group interaction can add excitement. Frequently, fresh ideas emerge that provide more practical applications to your concepts.

As part of your preparation, write these words at the top of a notepad: "Questions for Small Group Discussion." Each question should focus on one of your main points. Then, as you move through your program, call for group discussions at the appropriate times.

FREQUENTLY, FRESH IDEAS EMERGE THAT PROVIDE MORE PRACTICAL APPLICATIONS TO YOUR CONCEPTS

4. Refer to Members of Your Audience

Mentioning a listener by name creates a powerful connection with the group. Some speakers gather significant information by interviewing several members of the audience before the program.

Celebrity speakers know that a reference to someone familiar to the group allows the audience to view the speaker as "one of us." I once watched the newly elected president of a trade association involve his listeners by projecting the photo of someone in the audience, with a quote below the photo. It worked like magic to capture attention.

5. Use Music

At an insurance company awards banquet, upbeat music was playing full blast as the "Agent of the Year" was introduced.

MUSIC CAN SET A MOOD, RELAX, MOTIVATE AND EXCITE

Music is an excellent way to involve your audience. It can set a mood, relax, motivate and excite. As you prepare your speech, think of a place where music might be appropriate. Remember, most music is under copyright. Check with ASCAP or BMI on the Internet for questions of clearance.

6. Ask Questions

Many effective presentations begin with the speaker asking questions of the audience. It forces people to start thinking about your message. For example:

- A corporate spokesperson may use the "test question" approach to demonstrate the solid commitment of the corporation to pollution control.
- A human resources expert on sexual misconduct in the workplace could provide a multiple-choice quiz on situations that could give rise to hostile work environment charges against corporations.

If you really know your topic and feel comfortable with a more flexible presentation, you can ask your audience questions you will answer during the session.

A trial attorney used this technique before a group of hostile insurance claims adjusters by asking them to answer this simple question: "When I leave here today, I finally want to understand why attorneys ____________." The claims adjusters verbally filled in the blank with several hard-hitting questions that they considered critical issues.

It was a learning experience for all involved – and a connection was made immediately with a difficult audience.

THIS BRIEF UNEXPECTED EXPRESSION OF THANKS ADDED HUMOR AND SPONTANEITY

7. Give Away Prizes

One association executive came prepared with several gifts and prizes she awarded to those who asked excellent questions. As you can imagine, there was no shortage of audience participation. This brief, unexpected expression of thanks added humor and spontaneity to her presentation.

8. Be Creative

IT WAS AMAZING HOW EASILY A BRAIN-STORMING SESSION WITH THE STAFF TRANSFORMED THE PROGRAM FROM A MONOTONOUS EXERCISE INTO AN EXCITING ONE

I conducted a workshop for a government agency whose staff was required to travel the state, providing "boring" (their words) information to the public. There was little enthusiasm for the program.

It was amazing how easily a brainstorming session with the staff transformed the program from a monotonous exercise into an exciting one. The staff members decided to use a game-show format in which audience members actually became contestants. Suddenly, the room was alive with ideas that would allow the staff to connect with members of the public.

You can add creative ways to involve your audience in every presentation. Take the time to discover them, and be willing to take risks.

ROB'S REMINDERS

- Motivate listeners to "talk back" mentally.
- Ask your audience for a physical response.
- Utilize small group discussions.
- Mention audience members by name.
- Ask meaningful questions.
- Find creative ways to involve your audience.

SHERMAN'S LAW #13

VARY TONE, INFLECTION AND VOLUME AND YOU'LL KEEP THEM RIVETED

What a thrill it is to listen to speakers who have mastered the art of voice control. At some moments during their delivery they speak quickly, then suddenly slow to a snail's pace to make an important point. They raise their voices to emphasize anger while telling a story, then speak in a whisper to capture your attention.

GREAT SPEAKERS UNDER-STAND THAT AN AUDIENCE CANNOT ABSORB A FAST-PACED 30-MINUTE SPEECH

PITCH, POWER, PACE

Great speakers understand that an audience cannot absorb a fast-paced 30-minute speech. Nor can they tolerate a program that does not include variations in voice tone. Changing your pitch, power and pace will keep the focus where it belongs:

on you and your subject.

Are you ready for a crash course in vocal improvement? Listen to an audiotape of one of your speeches and ask yourself these six questions:

1. Do I vary the pitch?

When it comes to pitch variance, speak naturally but deliberately add highs and lows. An "annoying" voice is one that usually stays at the same level without changing. It is monotone, either high or low, shrill or booming. The audience complains because of the *sameness* – it is boring. Could you endure a singer who stayed on one note for the entire song?

SPEAK NATURALLY, BUT DELIBERATELY ADD HIGHS AND LOWS

Some people believe they should develop a deep, resonant voice, and as a result they speak with low energy and little enthusiasm. Others try over inflecting, which can sound artificial rather than believable.

Listen closely and you may detect an unwanted speech pattern, such as raising the pitch of your voice at the end of sentences. This is a sign of looking for approval – a killer in speech and in life.

2. Do I vary the rate?

Do you know your speaking rate? Choose any 140 words on this page and read them out loud. It should take 60 seconds. Read those words again until you reach this pace. That's your starting point. Now learn to vary your speed as the situation requires.

Thoughtful comments demand speech that is slow and solemn. At a sales rally, however, you'd better pick up the speed. It's your change of pace that results in interest and emphasis.

Until I began analyzing my tapes, I was a rapid-fire speaker – constantly. Once I heard myself I thought, "If I'm having a hard time processing this information, it must be even more difficult for my audience." I slowed down and began to add variety.

WHEN YOU WANT TO MAKE A POINT, SPEAK LOUDER AND SLOWER OR SOFTER AND SLOWER. CHANGE THE WAY YOU SPEAK.

– RON ARDEN

3. Do I vary the volume?

All words cannot have equal value. Some are transitions or "preparatory words" leading to something of significance. Place the power where it belongs.

Here's a drill. Say this sentence out loud: "We must finish this race." Now repeat it five times, each with an emphasis on a different word. Do you see how volume – or power – can change the meaning?

A word of caution. Avoid getting into patterns, such as stressing a word in approximately the same place in every sentence. Also learn to use a microphone like a pro. Stand back when you're loud; lean toward it when your speech is soft.

4. Am I speaking clearly?

Practice reading aloud, making every syllable count. Now attempt to accomplish the same thing when you stand before a group.

Have you ever noticed that some speakers actually cut off the final syllable of many words? As a result, the message is garbled.

Learn to articulate. It helps to stand in front of a mirror to be sure you have plenty of jaw action – and that your lips are really moving. Many in your audience are "lip reading." It's part of the communication process.

PSYCHO-LOGICALLY, SOME PEOPLE ARE AFRAID THAT IF THEY STOP TALKING – EVEN FOR A MOMENT – THEIR LISTENERS MIGHT LEAVE THE ROOM

Here's an interesting technique for improving your articulation: Place a cork from a wine bottle between your teeth and practice sounds such as "be, ba, bow, ce, ca, can, so, de, da, dan, do." This will exercise the muscles needed for articulation, and you'll notice the improvement.

5. Am I using unnecessary "fillers?"

Most novice speakers have no idea how many times they use "um," "uh," "you know," or "okay" as *fillers* in their delivery.

They're used to fill space between thoughts. Psychologically, some people are afraid that if they stop talking – even for a moment – their listeners might leave the room.

Do you realize that some audience members actually start tabulating the number of times you use one of these nonwords? After your address, the only thing they can remember is how many times you said "uh" or "um."

Tape yourself again and again until you have totally eliminated these annoying fillers. What do you replace them with? Silence!

6. Do I add enough pauses?

What's the best advice to a speaker whose train of thought has suddenly derailed? Instead of cluttering the wreckage with more words, *pause*. Let your previous thoughts sink in. The audience will think it's on purpose.

Silence is a speaker's best friend. Don't be afraid to stop talking and allow "quiet" to engulf the room. People cannot process words as quickly as they are spoken. Give your listeners that time.

One speaker told me, "After an important point I pause and silently count from one to three – to let the concept sink in." If you try it, those three seconds will

PAUSES MAKE YOU APPEAR TO BE ASSERTIVE AND IN CONTROL

– JO ROBBINS

seem like an eternity, yet they add power.

On your note cards write the word "PAUSE" where you think it is needed. Or write the words "SILENCE" or "SLOW DOWN" at the top and bottom of each card as a reminder.

With practice, you'll begin to *hear* the punctuation marks, and automatically add them as you speak.

VARIETY – IT'S THE SPICE OF SPEAKING!

LESS IS MORE

Learn to constantly "read" your audience. Know when it's time to either raise your voice, speak softly or add something dramatic.

Speaker Betsy Buckley says, "I pause. I lower my voice. I'll even whisper. For me, holding attention means being more quiet, since silence seems to encourage them to become more involved. Less from me often equals more from them."[1]

Variety – it's the spice of speaking!

ROB'S REMINDERS

- Speak naturally, but vary your pitch.
- Change your pace according to the content.
- Add variety to your power and volume.
- Articulate! Make every syllable count.
- Replace "fillers" with silence.
- A pause can produce applause.

SHERMAN'S LAW #14

NO LANGUAGE IS AS EFFECTIVE AS BODY LANGUAGE

Gestures and body movement are like spices in a soup – they can either add or distract, depending on how much you use.

Movement is important for two reasons:

- It helps you to relax and adds energy to your speech.
- It causes listeners to pay closer attention to both you and your message.

How important is your body language? Speech coach Patricia Fripp says, "An audience doesn't remember what you say. They remember what they see."[1]

AN AUDIENCE DOESN'T REMEMBER WHAT YOU SAY. THEY REMEMBER WHAT THEY SEE

– PATRICIA FRIPP

WHAT YOU ARE SPEAKS SO LOUDLY, I CANNOT HEAR WHAT YOU SAY

–RALPH WALDO EMERSON

ARE YOU GUILTY?

You will never correct distracting habits unless you are fully aware of them. Closely examine a video of your presentation and place a check mark on any of the following:

- ❑ I'm rattling coins or keys in my pocket.
- ❑ I'm twisting my ring.
- ❑ I'm standing too rigid.
- ❑ I'm rocking from side to side.
- ❑ I'm playing with my watch.
- ❑ I'm drumming my fingers on the lectern.
- ❑ I'm blowing the hair out of my eyes.
- ❑ I'm licking my lips.
- ❑ I'm constantly pushing up the bridge of my glasses.
- ❑ Woman: I'm playing with my jewelry, or twirling my hair.
- ❑ Man: I'm stroking my beard.
- ❑ Oh no! I'm chewing gum!

SHERMAN'S SUGGESTIONS

As you gain experience as a speaker, you'll become more aware of your body language. As part of that process, here are seven important things to remember:

1. Don't hang on to the lectern.

Some speakers seem glued to the lectern, clenching it with both hands as if it were a life preserver in a storm-tossed ocean. Use it as a tool, not a crutch. Better yet, come out from behind the lectern during your speech.

2. Avoid swaying or repetitive patterns of movement.

If you find yourself starting to sway, take one or two steps and stop, standing with your weight distributed evenly on both feet.

Imagine that your heels are held by roots in the ground. Don't take one step unless it is intentional and tied to some change in concept. Now look into someone's eyes. Begin to make your point and walk toward that person a few steps. Stop and plant your heels, and don't move again until you are ready to make another point.

Also become aware of – and eliminate – any "repeating" motion, such as finger pointing or rubbing your hands together.

3. Keep your hands free and your palms open.

Don't clench your fist, use the "fig-leaf" stance of placing your hands in a "V" over your crotch area, or hold both hands at chest level, as if you are in prayer. It's best for both hands to remain empty, at your side, raising them to gesture when it is appropriate.

Patricia Ball, a noted presentation skills coach, says, "Keep your palms visible. Hands held forward with palms up convey sincerity and openness."[2]

When you are using a handheld mike, keep using gestures with your free hand.

KEEP YOUR PALMS VISIBLE. HANDS HELD FORWARD WITH PALMS UP CONVEY SINCERITY AND OPENNESS.

– PATRICIA BALL

4. Let your gestures reflect your thoughts.

Time your movements so they mirror your most important words. For example, if you say, "It's all in your mind," point to your temple.

TIME YOUR MOVEMENTS SO THEY MIRROR YOUR MOST IMPORTANT WORDS

Descriptive gestures help your listeners visualize size, shape, location or movement. *Suggestive gestures* convey feeling, emotion and attitude – such as frowning or shrugging your shoulders.

5. Stand tall!

Don't slouch. It will drain the energy from both you and your audience. As you speak, keep thinking, "Stand tall! Stand tall!" It may help to imagine your breastbone is attached to strings and someone is pulling it up.

6. Make your movements deliberate.

Every gesture should be purposeful. When you move from the lectern, don't just walk one step – it makes you seem hesitant and unsure of yourself. Instead, take two or three steps at a time. And remember, *larger crowds require larger gestures*.

7. Let your clothes communicate.

What you wear is part of your body language. Dress conservatively in quality clothing – dark blue or black are the preferred choices. Shine your shoes.

Men: Wear a white or blue dress shirt (not button-down) and a "quiet" tie. Dress one level "above" your audience. You can dress more informally if it is a casual event, but your clothes should always be fastidiously pressed and classy.

Women: Wear solid color dresses or "office" suits. Avoid excessive jewelry, makeup or extreme hair styles. Try wearing "jewel tone" jackets and black shirts for a combination of power and energy.

A note of caution: Many backdrops are black, and if you are projected onto a large screen wearing black, you will appear lost.

AVOID DISTRACTIONS

I've been asked, "What should I do if I can't keep my hands still and they become a distraction?"

Until you eliminate needless nervous habits, try holding something in your hand, such as a paper clip, one of your note cards, a handout, or, best of all, a handheld microphone. It will bring some temporary *steadiness*. Your long-term goal, however, is to keep your hands free so that you can use meaningful, proper gestures.

YOUR LONGTERM GOAL IS TO KEEP YOUR HANDS FREE SO THAT YOU CAN USE MEANINGFUL, PROPER GESTURES

SPEAK INTO THE MIKE

Often you will be asked whether you prefer a hand-held microphone, a clip-on wireless lavaliere, or a mike attached to the lectern. Each has its advantages, and – and you must decide what's best for you:

- The wireless clip-on leaves you free to walk around and use both hands for gestures, but you can't control volume. Also, sound quality often suffers with a wireless mike.
- The handheld microphone allows you to control the volume by the distance you place it from your mouth. However, you have only one hand free for gestures.
- The stationary microphone frees both hands and lets you control the volume, but prohibits walking around.

NOTE: If you use either a handheld or stationary microphone, be sure it is placed just beneath your mouth. You'll avoid "popping" sounds and people can see your facial expressions.

YOU'RE NOT SEEKING PERFECTION, BUT NATURALNESS

When you speak naturally, gestures and movement will flow easily and authentically.

ROB'S REMINDERS

- Become aware of your distracting habits.
- Keep both hands free.
- Gestures should mirror your thoughts.
- Make your movements deliberate.
- Dress conservatively.
- Don't seek perfection, but naturalness.

SHERMAN'S LAW #15

LOOK THEM IN THE EYE

When I first started speaking, I had trouble looking into the eyes of my listeners. I'd stare at my notes, glance at my audiovisuals and peer into the distance – as if the audience was somewhere else. On my early evaluation forms, the same advice kept appearing, "Establish more eye contact." I made that adjustment.

Can you imagine a one-on-one conversation with no eye contact? Speaking to a group is no different. The same connection is required.

When you look directly at one person you are saying, "You are important to me."

TO MAKE ONESELF UNDER-STOOD TO PEOPLE, ONE MUST FIRST SPEAK TO THEIR EYES

- NAPOLEON

MAKING CONTACT

If you want to establish rapport, start using

these nine eye-opening keys:

1. Don't talk to your notes or to your visual aids.

If you look at your notes, read from printed materials, or concentrate on a visual aid for as few as 10 seconds, the connection you have established with the audience can be lost. One speaker told me, "When I look down, I pause. Then I re-establish eye contact with someone and continue speaking."

2. Start seeing friends.

My visual link with the audience is greatly improved when I take the time to greet as many people as possible prior to the program. Why? It is much easier to speak to friends than to strangers.

DON'T USE THE MACHINE-GUN APPROACH, HURRIEDLY SCANNING THE ROOM

3. Use the three-second rule.

Don't use the machine-gun approach, hurriedly scanning the room with your eyes darting from side to side. Take your time. Look at one individual for about three seconds, or until you've finished your sentence or thought. Then move on.

4. Look at many, not a few.

Avoid looking at the same few people again and again. And don't fix your gaze on one particular part of the room.

5. Don't stare.

To avoid the appearance that you are staring at someone, try looking at *one* eye of an audience member, rather than directly into both eyes.

6. Find a smiling face.

If things aren't going well, look at a friendly face until the momentary problem has passed.

7. Don't worry about large groups.

If you're in a big auditorium, practice the same one-on-one techniques. One speaker said, "I start in the back, and zig-zag my way forward, looking directly into the eyes of individuals along the way."

8. Practice making your eyes expressive.

What do people see when they look directly into your eyes? Make sure they are expressive. If you are excited, open them wide. If you are being thoughtful or pensive, narrow them.

9. Look for feedback.

There's no better indicator of audience attention than their eyes. It's the only way to know if they understand you, or if you're speaking too fast or too slowly. Just look – you'll have instant feedback.

THERE'S NO BETTER INDICATOR OF AUDIENCE ATTENTION THAN THEIR EYES

EYE CONTACT SAYS, "YOU ARE IMPORTANT!"

ROB'S REMINDERS

- Eye contact says, "You are important!"
- Meet audience members before you speak.
- Don't talk to your notes, talk to people.
- Look at each individual for about three seconds.
- Search for friendly faces.
- Eye contact gives instant feedback.

SHERMAN'S LAW #16

SPEAKERS ARE ARTISTS WHO PAINT WITH PICTURES

As a trial attorney, I know the power of painting word pictures.

Although the art of storytelling in the courtroom has decreased in recent years, it is still dramatic and effective.

A friend told me about a lawyer who, in his deep southern drawl, recounted the life of his disabled child-plaintiff. He described how "his home looked like every other home in the area, except for the wheelchair ramps that had to be installed because of this tragic accident." His voice choked with emotion as he related how the bathroom cabinets and sink had to be lowered to accommodate this disabled child.

IF THE AUDIENCE IS TO VISUALIZE WHAT YOU ARE SAYING, YOU MUST FIRST VISUALIZE YOUR IDEAS

- KIRK KIRKPATRICK

Jurors began to wipe the tears from their eyes and, during a break, the opposing side asked to settle the case.

CAN THEY *SEE* IT?

Here are four ways that stories, illustrations and anecdotes can make your presentation come alive:

PROFESSIONAL SPEAKERS KNOW THAT WHAT THEY'VE LEARNED FROM LIFE'S LESSONS WILL HELP THEM BOND WITH THE AUDIENCE

1. Relate personal experiences.

Any concept is easier to understand if it is punctuated by your own experiences. Personal stories are especially powerful if they reveal your human frailties and weaknesses. Professional speakers know that what they've learned from life's lessons will help them bond with the audience.

If you have a choice between telling a story that happened to someone else or one that happened to you, use the personal account. The audience wants to relate to *you* – not the childhood experiences of Winston Churchill or Albert Einstein. A short quote or a brief life encounter of a noted person might support a key theme, but move on quickly.

Also, your listeners don't want a rehash of *Chicken Soup for the Soul.* It's *your* story they came to hear.

2. Keep your stories short.

Rambling narratives will turn off your

audience. They'll be thinking, "Okay, make your point!"

Most presentations work better with several short stories inserted at appropriate places rather than one long saga.

3. Tie every story to your theme.

If an illustration has no relevance to a major point you're making, don't use it. It's a lesson I learned the hard way.

I once shared a wonderful account (wonderful to me) of my experiences coaching underprivileged children through a local community organization. The story was fun to tell, but it left my audience asking, "So what?"

Celebrity speakers often make the same mistake. They love to relate behind-the-scenes stories about moviemaking, politics or sports, yet there is often no rhyme or reason for the anecdote.

The football player or beauty pageant winner needs to relate obstacles they have overcome and link them to their listeners, perhaps saying, "In the same way, you can reach your goals."

In your preparation, ask yourself again and again, "What's the major point of this story, and how does it relate to my theme?"

A word of caution: Avoid the temptation to use the platform as a form of self-therapy. This is not the time to work through a family crisis.

ASK YOURSELF AGAIN AND AGAIN, "WHAT'S THE MAJOR MESSAGE OF THIS STORY?"

4. Create vivid word images.

Select key words you want people to remember, and then attach vivid word pictures people can visualize.

Don't just say, "I was really afraid." Rather, use "The fear left me numb, as if I was paralyzed." Instead of saying, "It was cold and the wind was blowing," try "My bones were freezing and the wind was howling in my ears."

Descriptive phrases will come easy if, after a key word, you add "like" or "as if" – and finish the sentence

5. Make a point, then tell a story.

One of the easiest ways to incorporate stories into your programs is to make a point, then tie a story to that point. The point/story, point/story approach is a simple way to organize your speech.

YOU'RE AN ARTIST START PAINTING!

You're an artist. Start painting!

ROB'S REMINDERS

- Use personal stories. They're powerful!
- Share what you've learned from life' lessons.
- Keep your stories short.
- Be sure your illustrations are relevant to your theme.
- Don't use the platform for self-therapy.
- Create vivid word images.

SHERMAN'S LAW #17

SPEAK TEN "YOU'S" FOR EVERY "I"

At a recent meeting of the National Speakers Association, platform per- sonality Joel Weldon demonstrated what "You Power" is all about. He actually gave the same speech twice. The first was peppered with "I's" and it received polite applause. Then he repeated his address, changing the wording to include "you" as many times as possible. What a dynamic turnaround! Weldon received a standing ovation.

Make a transcript of your most recent presentation. Now circle every "I" and every "you." What is the ratio? If it's not ten to one in favor of "you," rewrite your speech.

HE THAT FALLS IN LOVE WITH HIMSELF WILL HAVE NO RIVALS

– BENJAMIN FRANKLIN

IT'S ABOUT *THEM!*

The speaker who is stuck in the "I" syndrome can quickly create an indifferent or even hostile audience. Listeners may turn the speaker off mentally, and even *physically*. Not only will they stop thinking along with you, but some will shift their bodies to the side or even close their eyes. These are sure signs they're distancing themselves from an ego-driven speaker.

MENTALLY YOU MUST TURN THE SPOTLIGHT ON THE AUDIENCE

While it's true that *you* are on stage, mentally you need to turn the spotlight on the audience. Keep telling yourself, "This speech is not about me – it's about *them!*"

To move your listeners forward, you must first establish common ground. Speech coach Ron Arden says, "A bond is created with the audience through similarities." He advises: "Talk about your commonalties with the audience."[1]

AN EMPHASIS ON "WE"

In the Gettysburg Address, which took Abraham Lincoln only three minutes to deliver, the emphasis was on "we," not "me." At the battleground cemetery he said, "Now we are engaged in a great civil war."

Lincoln, in the oft-quoted speech, used "we" ten times and "us" three times – but not once did he utter the word "I." Perhaps that's why we laud it as such a memorable event.

Nearly a century later, on January 20, 1961, John Kennedy delivered his famous inaugural address. The words we most remember focused on "you." He said, "And so, my fellow Americans: ask not what your country can do for you – ask what you can do for your country."

In that text, Kennedy used the word "I" only four times. Yet he included "we," "us," "our," "you" or "your" 51 times. That's even *more* than the ten-to-one ratio.

Mike Frank, professional speaker and speaker bureau owner, cautions people not to overuse the word "you." Says Frank, "It can often come across as preaching." He prefers sprinkling in "we" to make it more acceptable and digestible.

ASK NOT WHAT YOUR COUNTRY CAN DO FOR YOU – ASK WHAT YOU CAN DO FOR YOUR COUNTRY

– JOHN F. KENNEDY

START REWRITING

Pay close attention to word structure. For example, the self-centered speaker says, "I think it is important to be involved in the community so that its goals are reached." The audience-centered speaker says, "You will find many opportunities if you get involved in your community. We must all work hard to help reach our goals."

Likewise, instead of saying, "Later I am going to tell you how I solved the problem," you would say, "Later we are going to find out how we can solve the problem together."

Be like the mouse who said to the elephant as they walked across a bridge, "Together we're shaking this thing."

WHEN YOU SING YOUR OWN PRAISES, YOU RARELY GET AN ENCORE

ROB'S REMINDERS

- Make a transcript and check your "I" –"you" ratio.
- Listeners turn off self-centered speakers.
- Direct the spotlight toward the audience.
- Establish common ground with your listeners.
- Great speakers place the emphasis on "we" and "you."
- Rewrite your speech to make it "audience centered."

SHERMAN'S LAW #18

ADD HUMOR TO BRING LIFE TO A SPEECH

To loosen up your audience, use humor like dynamite – carefully and in the right places!

What are the benefits of humor?

- It's an icebreaker.
- It relieves tension.
- It creates rapport with the audience.
- It gives listeners a breathing spell.
- It produces an atmosphere for communication.

Even more, it has been proven that information delivered in a "light" or entertaining form is remembered longer than more seriously delivered material.

USE HUMOR LIKE DYNAMITE – CAREFULLY AND IN THE RIGHT PLACES!

MAKE IT WORK!

As you prepare for your speech, remember these six principles:

1. Humor must be relevant.

Where is it written that every presentation must begin with an introductory joke that has no relevance to the topic? I am sure you have endured too many speeches that began with a meaningless joke. It's a mistake you should avoid. Also consider that if the joke bombs, you have created a distraction you must now overcome.

Humor is an important ingredient, but it must be fitting and appropriate to your theme.

2. Don't use "canned" jokes.

Your objective is to communicate with a sense of humor – not to relate tired stories. Tony Alessandra, marketing strategist and professional speaker, says, "When you tell jokes you've heard before, you run the risk of telling one or more to an audience who's already heard them as well."[1] That's a recipe for disaster.

ALWAYS CHECK THE EXPIRATION DATES ON OLD JOKES!

Always check the expiration dates on old jokes!

You will rarely go wrong choosing stories based on real-life experiences.

3. Humor must flow.

Don't try to "force" an anecdote, quote or one-liner into your presentation. Humor must flow naturally and not be seen as an appendage.

Also, don't promise a laugh by saying, "Let me tell you a funny story." Your audience may suddenly be on the defensive.

As you become more comfortable, humor will seem spontaneous and become a part of your style. Relax. Let it happen naturally.

4. Tell stories about yourself.

What are the tales you tell your friends about your past? If they are relevant to a point you're making, add them. Even relating something that is personally embarrassing or revealing can work. However, make sure your accounts are not boastful or self-serving.

Terry Paulson, former president of the National Speakers Association, uses this technique to perfection. Terry will often relate an entertaining story from his past in which he took one step backward to move two steps forward. The connection with his audience is immediate.

A LAUGH IS WORTH A HUNDRED GROANS IN ANY MARKET

– CHARLES LAMB

5. Keep your humor short.

There's nothing more boring than a long, drawn-out, awkward narrative. If you are making a decision between a one-liner and a longer anecdote, choose the one-liner.

One of the great dangers of a long story is that it may bomb – and you're the one who will be shell-shocked. To reduce the risk, make sure the humor reinforces a major point of your address.

6. Never use sexist, racist, ethnic or off-color humor.

IF YOU HAVE THE SLIGHTEST FEELING THAT YOUR MATERIAL MAY BE OFFENSIVE, THROW IT OUT

If you have the slightest feeling that your material may be offensive, throw it out. There's a long list of broadcasters, executives, and celebrities whose ill-chosen words have returned like a boomerang.

The fact that you're Italian doesn't give you a license to tell Italian jokes. Someone is sure to be offended.

TIMING AND PACE

One of the secrets to delivering humor effectively is not to become too loud, speak too fast, or become too aggressive. As speaker Paul Seaburn says, "Wit requires timing and pace, and the punctuation mark which provides this is the comma, the sign of the pause. Use plenty of commas when you write the humor segments of your speech, especially right before the punch lines, and remember to pause at those points in your delivery."

Some speakers have great material, yet they don't give the audience enough time to laugh. With experience comes pacing, timing and a "rhythm" that allows your humor to have maximum impact.

"THE CHILI PEPPER"

You may shrug your shoulders and say, "Rob, I'm just not a funny person. What should I do?"

Smile! Show your pearly whites! A smile is the chili pepper of public speaking. No matter how grave your subject, a sudden smile can punch a point across.

A SMILE IS THE CHILI PEPPER OF PUBLIC SPEAKING

A few well-placed chuckles sprinkled here and there with a smile on your face is all that is needed to get you moving in the right direction.

My friend Phil Sorentino, founder of Humor Consultants and longtime professional speaker, is often asked where he gets his humor. Phil replies, "I follow me around and take notes."

ROB'S REMINDERS

- Humor must be relevant.
- Don't use "canned" jokes.
- Humor must flow.
- Tell stories about yourself.
- Keep your humor short.
- Never use sexist, racist, ethnic or
- off-color material.

SHERMAN'S LAW #19

FOR A POWERFUL PRESENTATION, ADD VISUAL IMPACT

Let's face the facts. We live in a visual age, and, as a speaker, you are in competition with MTV, Disney and the best New York or Hollywood has to offer.

Sure, I've seen excellent speakers hold an audience spellbound without one prop or graphic. Today, however, listener expectations almost *demand* that certain types of presentations use visuals. For example, addressing a sales and marketing workshop is much different than standing before a parent-teacher meeting.

Well-designed visuals help the audience feel more comfortable. They know you have a plan and are following it. Graphics also keep people awake by stimulating their senses.

THINGS SEEN ARE MIGHTIER THAN THINGS HEARD

-ALFRED LORD TENNYSON

TWO THINGS TO REMEMBER ABOUT VISUAL AIDS: NUMBER ONE, THEY SHOULD BE VISUAL. NUMBER TWO, THEY SHOULD AID.

– ALLATIA HARRIS

The good news is that you don't need a Hollywood producer to provide "value" to your audience through visual and audio aids. You can choose from many mediums to add impact to your presentation.

HANDOUTS

A simple handout is a good place to start. Speakers use handouts differently. Some pass them out at the beginning, some *during* the program, and others at the end.

Some speakers fear that people will read ahead and not pay attention to what is being said if handouts are provided in advance. Consider a "fill-in-the-blank" handout requiring listeners to actively follow along, writing down key words and concepts. Some speakers use shades of colored paper for multiple handouts. It's easy to say, "Look at your yellow handout."

However, you must know your audience when considering handouts. For instance, a group of CEOs may balk at a fill-in-the-blank handout. And a five-page handout distributed during a dinner event would probably remain on the table.

FLIP CHARTS

Flip charts are another simple tool than can enliven your program.

- Write only on the top two-thirds of the sheet for easy viewing.
- Use extra thick markers.

- Use black or blue markers with red or green for emphasis.
- Don't use too many words per page.

Many speakers prepare the sheets in advance so they don't have to turn their back to the audience as they write. Consider asking an audience member to write on the chart if your visuals are more spontaneous. Also, try using a blank sheet between each page. That way, during transitions, the message is not in competition with you.

OVERHEAD PROJECTORS

Of all visual aids, the "overhead" is still the workhorse of the industry.

Some speakers cover the transparency with a solid sheet of paper and move it down the screen as they reveal each point. Others mask out everything but the item they are discussing.

- Place the screen high enough for people to see, but not so elevated that you have a "keystone" effect with some words out of focus.
- Never speak to the screen. Look at the visual, pause, turn back to the audience and begin speaking.

An effective use of an overhead is to place a clear transparency over the one you have prepared. Then use a dry-erase marker to check off highlighted items or circle (or underline) words or numbers as you talk about them.

PLACE THE SCREEN ON THE RIGHT OR LEFT. THE CENTER IS RESERVED FOR THE FEATURE ATTRACTION: YOU!

SLIDE SHOWS

The quality of color transparencies can add a professional touch to your session. They are especially effective with large audiences or when photos are needed.

- Place the screen for the overhead or slide projector on the right or left side of the platform. The center is reserved for the feature attraction: *you!*
- You can also solve a lighting problem by using a small cameo spotlight, which allows the audience to see both you and the screen in a darkened room.
- Your visuals can contain words, diagrams, graphs, or charts.

I TOSSED MY DAUGHTER'S PLAY DUCK INTO THE AIR AND USED HER SQUIRT GUN TO SHOOT IT DOWN

PROPS

I once gave a presentation to a state agency on consensus building among diverse stakeholders. To emphasize how poorly we make decisions in state government, I used an analogy developed by employer representative Jim Palmer. I explained that constituency groups frequently try to influence government decision-making by unilaterally developing their own ideas. These ideas become "ducks" that are shot at by other constituency groups. To illustrate the point, I tossed my daughter's play duck into the air and used her squirt gun to shoot it down.

Using props is risky, but their effect

can be long lasting. Why not have a little fun with "dry" presentations? You'll be remembered!

LCD PROJECTORS

The lowered cost and increased clarity of LCD projectors have enhanced their popularity with speakers. The computer-driven projector turns an overhead into an animated, colorful visual display. When combined with the software of Microsoft PowerPoint®, Harvard Graphics®, or Corel Presentation™, the possibilities are as varied as your imagination.

However, don't allow your visuals to be the tail that wags the dog. The graphics should illustrate your point, not steal the show.

YOU ARE "LARGER THAN LIFE" AND AUDIENCE MEMBERS CLOSELY SCRUTINIZE EVERY MOVEMENT

IMAGE MAGNIFICATION

At large functions, your image is likely to be projected on a big screen. Remember, you are "larger than life" and audience members closely scrutinize every movement.

One business speaker took a drink of water just before he spoke and then spit the ice into the glass. There was an audible gasp from the audience as they watched his actions on the enormous TV screen. The speaker lost credibility before his first word.

- Be careful of high-contrasting clothing or jewelry. White-against-black clothing can cause a glare.
- Use smaller gestures when people are watching a large screen. Your

movements are magnified.

- Meet ahead of time with the production crew regarding any unique elements of your presentation.

POINTS FROM THE PROS

DON'T JUST SAY IT, LET PEOPLE SEE IT

Most professionals stick to fewer than 10 words per graphic. One speaker says, "I limit my material to the amount of information I would place on a sweatshirt."

Some speakers are totally opposed to words on visuals, believing they are redundant. Instead, they limit their graphics to photos and illustrations that add strength to a concept.

The real pros talk about the visual before showing it – much like saying, "That's my point, now I want to show you the evidence."

Don't just say it, let people *see* it.

ROB'S REMINDERS

- Speak to your listeners, not to the visual.
- Be sure the audience can see both you and the graphic.
- Don't use complex visual aids. Keep it simple.
- Enliven your program with props.
- Place screens to your right or left. You are the center attraction.
- Let visuals support your words, not dominate the presentation.

SHERMAN'S LAW #20

NEVER END WITH QUESTIONS AND ANSWERS

Resist the temptation to conclude your presentation with a question-and-answer period. Why? During Q&A, you often have little control over content and direction.

Barb Wingfield of Morale Builders suggests that your speech should end strong! A question-and-answer session often ends with a whimper. Instead, allot a specific time – say 10 minutes – for questions, then move into a strong, pre-planned conclusion.

Your transition into the questions can let the audience know there is more to follow. Say, "Let's take time for a few questions and answers before we conclude today's program."

By structuring your presentation this way, you gain audience input, address

YOUR SPEECH SHOULD END STRONG! A QUESTION AND-ANSWER SESSION OFTEN ENDS WITH A WHIMPER

critical concerns, and end powerfully by reinforcing the purpose of your speech.

Studies show that the ability of an average audience to focus dramatically declines after about 20 minutes. That's why so many excellent speakers move into question-answer sessions at about the 20-minute mark. As one platform personality said, "Why fight human nature? If they're going to fall asleep, I've got to take countermeasures."

TWELVE Q&A GUIDELINES

LISTEN – REALLY LISTEN – TO EVERY WORD OF THE QUESTIONER

If you want to have a successful question-and-answer session, follow these 12 guidelines:

1. **Give the questioner full eye contact and attention.** Listen – *really* listen – to every word. Professionals often lean forward to show their interest.
2. **Don't interrupt and attempt to finish the question.** You could be embarrassed when the person says, "That's not what I am asking."
3. **Always repeat the question so that everyone hears it.** This gives you time to better formulate your answer.

4. **If you know the questioner's name, use it.** In small groups, you may be able to read the person's name badge. It creates a great rapport with the audience.
5. **Pause before giving your answer.** This lets the listeners know you're reflecting on the question.
6. **Compliment the questioner.** Use phrases such as "Excellent question" or "I appreciate that question."
7. **Keep your answers brief.** This isn't the time for another speech.
8. **As you give your answer, let your eye contact move from the questioner to the entire audience.** Bring everyone into the dialogue. Continuing to look at the questioner may give the person the opportunity to argue with you.
9. **If you do not know the answer, don't bluff.** People don't expect you to know *everything*. Simply say, "I don't know," or "I don't have the answer, but if you'll give me your card or e-mail address after the program, I will research it and get back to you."
10. **Refer back to your presentation.** Let the questions reinforce the major points of your address.
11. **Mention your experience on the topic.** Let people know that you are speaking from firsthand knowledge.

LET THE QUESTIONS REINFORCE THE MAJOR POINTS OF YOUR ADDRESS

12. Don't allow questions to drift off topic. Say, "I'd love to discuss that with you after the program. Will you remain a few minutes so we can talk?"

REFLECTIVE LISTENING

If you are asked a question that requires skill in answering, use the "reflective listening" technique. You *reflect back* the question by repeating it in a way that shows you understand it. For example, respond with, "What I hear you saying is . . . ." Then, in your own words, repeat what the person has said. This technique is widely used in negotiation and conflict resolution situations.

One speaker, when faced with a difficult query, turned to the audience for the answer. "Let me open this up," he said, "How would you deal with this issue?"

HONOR AND RESPECT

ANY ATTEMPT TO MAKE THE QUESTIONER LOOK BAD WILL BACKFIRE

Over time, you're going to run into rude, obnoxious, even incomprehensible questioners. Don't mirror their attitude. Treat every person with honor, dignity and respect. Remember, there is no such thing as a dumb question. Any attempt to make the person look bad will backfire.

You may encounter people who want to

grandstand and give their own speech during the Q&A. Don't be shy about interrupting them with a smile on your face as you say, "I do apologize for interrupting, but we only have an hour here and I can see that we are losing people. I need you to drive right now to the point." The audience will love you for it.

GETTING STARTED

Think in advance, "What questions will likely be asked?" Prepare your answers, and wow your audience with a quote or statistic.

Some speakers will "plant" a question with a friend in the audience just in case the Q&A session gets off to a slow start.

If the crowd is quiet, ask *yourself* a question: "Earlier today I was asked . . . ." You may even solicit written questions in advance. Have them collected and choose the ones you wish to answer.

At times you may need to reword a question to lead you where you want to go. Phrases to accomplish that purpose include, "I think the real issue is . . . ," "In the larger context your question becomes . . . ," or "What your question seems to focus on is . . . ."

YOU DON'T HAVE TO KNOW ALL THE ANSWERS! BUT YOU DO NEED TO ALWAYS ADDRESS THE QUESTIONS

– TONY JEARY

With a little practice, you'll look forward to the question-and-answer session as a challenging and rewarding time.

ROB'S REMINDERS

- Questions and answers should come *before* a strong, planned conclusion.
- Give the questioner your complete attention.
- Compliment every questioner.
- If you don't know the answer, say so.
- Practice "reflective listening."
- Treat every person with honor, dignity and respect.

SHERMAN'S LAW #21

FINISH WITH A BANG!

Like a great fireworks show, you save your best for last. Yes, you begin with great attention-getting material, but the "big bang" is for the finish.

In most cases, a great presentation concludes by inspiring others to action. For example, you may motivate an audience to make a contribution to a special project, volunteer to participate in your organization or community event, or demonstrate the principles you've taught.

It is amazing how many speakers present excellent programs yet fail to conclude with a challenge. At the beginning of my speaking career, I made that mistake. I felt satisfied that I left my audience asking for more. Unfortunately, "asking for more" was really a euphemism for failing to convey a clear picture of what I wanted my listeners to do.

BEGIN WITH GREAT ATTENTION-GETTING MATERIAL, BUT THE "BIG BANG" IS FOR THE FINISH

HAPPY OR SERIOUS?

Noted speaker Tom Antion believes in using humor during the closing. Says Tom, "If you leave them laughing and applauding . . . an extremely positive impression about you will remain." However, if your entire speech has included humor, Tom advises that you finish seriously. He says, "This contrast will create a great impact. It will convey the fact that you believe in a lighthearted approach to the subject, but the results are very serious to you."[1]

WORD FOR WORD!

GET TO YOUR ENDING BEFORE THEY EXPECT IT!

In Law #11 I suggested that you may want to memorize the first 30 seconds of your presentation. You might also want to consider memorizing your close.

To some people, "finally" is the sweetest word you will speak. Surprise them – get to your ending before they expect it! Finish clearly and with authority; then take your seat. Leave the flowery thanks and acknowledgments to others.

Also remember:

- Be sure your finale mirrors and relates to your original purpose. It lets the audience know you satisfied that objective.
- Have only one ending. I've heard speakers use two or three conclusions that left the audience confused.

- End confidently. Never say, "That's about it," "And one more thing," or "Oh, I forgot to mention . . . ."

CLOSING CHOICES

Here are nine effective *closes* to consider:

1. **Tie the ribbon.** A finish that loops back to your opening presents a completed package.
2. **Summarize.** With fresh words, give a condensed review of your major points.
3. **Use humor.** Tell an entertaining story that drives home your theme.
4. **Use emotion.** Relate a heart-touching anecdote that illustrates your major point.
5. **Give a quotation.** Use a powerful quote people will long remember.
6. **Ask questions.** Pose a series of questions designed to make listeners think seriously about the topic.
7. **Ask for help.** Request that people join you in a cause.
8. **Give your opinion.** Speak candidly about your topic, even making predictions of what the future will hold.
9. **Issue a challenge.** Take the opportunity to inspire others to action.

Ask audience members what they plan to do differently as a result of your speech. This allows them to summarize your presentation and leaves everyone with a positive burst of energy as a close.

TAKE THE OPPORTUNITY TO INSPIRE OTHERS TO ACTION

CUTTING IT SHORT?

I've often been asked, "What happens if the program runs late and I'm given just 20 minutes to deliver a 40-minute speech?"

My advice is to end your presentation at the precise moment you are expected to – or even *before*. If your time has been shortened, start cutting material from the middle of your speech, but never from your prepared conclusion. And *never* apologize for the lack of time that remains for you to speak. Apologizing places the organizer of the event in an awkward position, and it makes you look bad.

PREPARE YOUR LISTENERS FOR THE CLOSE. IT MAKES THEM FEEL MORE COMFORT-ABLE.

"IN CONCLUSION"

Avoid saying "In conclusion." These words only trigger the "off" switch in your listener's minds. However, you do need to let people know you are approaching the end.

I learned a valuable lesson about closing from one of my first presentations. When it came time to conclude my talk, I just stopped – and people weren't sure if I was taking a long pause or if I had really finished. So after a few seconds of silence, I said, "Thank you very much for this opportunity to speak with you."

During my evaluation I was told, "Some-how, prepare the audience for the close. It makes them feel more comfortable."

How can you accomplish this? Use phrases such as, "Here's a story that brings it all into focus," or, "Before I close, let me illustrate what I mean by exceptional customer service." Or, say, "I want to leave you with the words of . . . ," and then give a memorable quote.

With practice, your tone of voice and rate of speech will signal that you are winding down.

One speaker, just before concluding, says, "I want to thank you for having me here today and for your kind attention. You've been a wonderful group," and then he goes into his close.

After your final words, take a long pause while your eyes survey the entire audience. Then say "Thank you."

End your speech as you started it: with a bang!

SCHOOL IS NEVER OUT FOR THE PRO

- CAVETT ROBERT

ROB'S REMINDERS

- Consider memorizing your conclusion.
- Your close must mirror your original purpose.
- Always end your program on time.
- Prepare your audience for the conclusion.
- Have only one ending, not two or three.
- Pause before your final words.

IT'S YOUR TIME TO SPEAK LIKE A LEADER

Every person with the ability to communicate can speak to any group. What stops us is our fear of the platform and the need for perfection.

It is my hope that through *Sherman's 21 Laws of Speaking* you realize that you don't have to be the perfect speaker. And I believe you now understand that your anxieties will diminish with practice and experience.

Give yourself permission to be yourself - even with your imperfections. You can bring value to any audience just by being well prepared and being *you!* Plus, if you make a contribution to the lives of others you will succeed despite your mistakes – especially if you show you care.

The opportunities available to enhance your executive skills through speaking to groups are abundant. When you inspire others to choose their own course consistent with your message, you powerfully demonstrate your leadership abilities.

People everywhere are thirsting for authentic leadership - and they are looking for ways to connect with you in a meaningful way. Start today to use the speaking skills you have learned. Take full advantage of your leadership talent and inspire others to action.

REFERENCES AND RESOURCES

REFERENCES

Introduction

1. David A. Peoples, *Presentation Plus* (New York: John Wiley & Sons, 1992), p. 6.
2. John Graham, "How to Win by Thinking Like a Listener," *American Salesman*, June 1, 1998, p. 7.

Law #1

1. Terry Pearce, *Leading Out Loud* (San Francisco: Jossey-Bass Publishers, 1995).
2. Morton C. Orman, M.D., *How to Conquer Public Speaking Fear,* Online at http://www.stresscure.com/jobstress/speak.html.
3. Lee Glickstein, *Be Heard Now* (New York: Broadway Books, 1998).
4. Granville N. Toogood, *The Articulate Executive* (New York: McGraw Hill, 1996), p. 29.

Law #2

1. Patrick Henry, quoted in Glenn R. Capp, *Famous Speeches in American History* (Indianapolis: Bobbs-Merrill Company, Inc., 1963), p. 23.
2. . Nido Qubein, *Communicate Like a Pro* (New York: Berkley Publishing, 1983), p. 219.

Law #3

1. A. L. "Kirk" Kirkpatrick, *Complete Speaker's and Toastmaster's Desk Book* (West Nyack, NY: Parker Publishing, 1981), p. 73.
2. Lee Glickstein, *Be Heard Now* (New York: Broadway Books, 1998).
3. Tony Jeary, *Inspire Any Audience* (Dallas, TX: Trophy Publishing, 1996), p. 88.

Law #4

1. Tony Jeary, *Inspire Any Audience* (Dallas, TX: Trophy Publishing, 1996), p. 16.

Law #5

1. Dottie Walters, *Speak and Grow Rich* (Englewood Cliffs, NJ: Prentice Hall, 1989), p. 19.

Law #6

1. Jo Robbins, *High Impact Presentations* (New York: John Wiley & Sons, Inc., 1997), p. 46.

Law #8 1. David A. Peoples, *Presentations Plus* (New York: John Wiley & Sons, Inc., 1992), p. 30.

Law #9 1. Steve Kissell, *Sharing Ideas*, Fall 1996, p. 16.

Law #10 1. Morton C. Orman, M.D., *How to Conquer Public Speaking Fear*, Online at http://www.stresscure.com/jobstress/speak.html.

Law #11 1. Joan Detz, "Delivery Plus Content Equals Successful Presentation," *Communication World*, April-May, 1998, p. 34.

Law #12 1. Nido Qubein, *Communicate Like a Pro* (New York: Berkley Books, 1983), p. 23.

Law #13 1. Betsy Buckley, *Professional Speaker*, July/August, 1999, p. 13.

Law #14 1. Patricia Fripp, National Speakers Association workshop, "Speaking Skills," October 9, 1999.

2. Patricia Ball, *Professional Speaker*, July/August, 1999, p. 8.

Law #17 1. Ron Arden, National Speakers Association workshop, "Speaking Skills," October 9, 1999.

Law #18 1. Tony Alessandra, *Professional Speaking*, July/August, 1999, p. 15.

Law #21 1. Tom Antion, *Sharing Ideas,* December/January, 1998, p. 36.

RESOURCES

The following Internet sites can be helpful in making your presentations more effective.

Antion, Tom: http://www.antion.com/TOC.htm
Fripp, Patricia: http://www.fripp.com
National Speakers Association: http://www.nsaspeaker.org
Ohio Speakers Forum: http://ohiospeakers.com
The Expertise Center: http://www.expertcenter.net/index.html
Toastmasters International: http://www.toastmasters.org
Speak and Grow Rich, Dottie and Lilly Walters:
http://www.experts.com/speak.html
Speakers Platform: http://www.speaking.com

ABOUT THE AUTHOR

ROB SHERMAN is an acclaimed speaker, author and attorney with a passion for helping people develop their leadership talent so they can inspire others to action.

Rob's presentations draw upon more than two decades of experience in business, law and association management. He is a graduate of the University of Cincinnati College of Law and spent six years with the Ohio Office of the Attorney General. He is a founding director of an adoption agency and also established a national real estate appraisal association. He has written on speaking and leadership skills for several national publications and has co-written two books on malpractice prevention strategies for doctors.

As president of the Sherman Leadership Group, he is an active member of the National Speakers Association and the Ohio Speakers Forum, and works with associations, corporations and CEOs as a consultant, presenter and executive trainer.

Rob is a principal with the law firm of Karr & Sherman, Co., L.P.A., in Columbus, Ohio, and is a visiting instructor at Otterbein College. He and his wife, Susan, are the parents of one daughter, Erin.

ACKNOWLEDGMENTS

This book is a culmination of the incredible talent of many individuals, including Winnie Ary, Cheryl Bassitt, Barbara Braham, Eric Burkland, Pat Campbell, Holly and Jim Canterucci, Lisa Crowe, John and Irene Dolan, Patrick Donadio, George Dunigan, Charles Dygert, Roxanne Emmerich, Gary Fetgatter, John Fleischman, Mike Frank, Paige Grant, Patti Hathaway, Gary Hoffman (cover art), Keith Karr, John Kengla, Mary Anne Knapke, C. Jacob Ladenheim, Wayne Lawson, Allen Liff, Diane Lukacsko, Pam Mitchel, Jim Palmer, Jack Park, Bill Petrarca, Angela Powell, Ed Rigsbee, Steve Rothrock, Walter Schaw, Susan Schubert, Phil Sorentino, Phil Stella, Danielle Turcola, Pat Vivo, Barb Wingfield and Lillian Zarzar.

Special thanks to my great friends at the National Speakers Association, Ohio Speakers Forum, American Society of Association Executives, Ohio State Chiropractic Association, and to my editor, Neil Eskelin.